北京指南
Beijing Official Guide

北京指南
Beijing Official Guide

主办：北京市人民政府新闻办公室　北京市旅游局
承制：北京月讯杂志社
北京对外文化交流中心
编委会主任：于长江、王惠、于德斌
编委会委员：王清、李雪敏
主编：刘开阳
常务副主编：章文舟
编辑部主任：孙幼庚
英文语言顾问：查尔斯·杜克斯
编辑：李婉、马乐、周航
图片编辑：姜波
美术设计及制作：王旭青、管力峰、刘杰、解星河
市场及销售总监：王琳
公关外联：许婧、方梅、付容
网络部：李飞扬、肖国斌、房蕾
发行：黄巍、聂涛
统一书号：ISBN 7-5085-0594-8
编辑部，销售部：中国北京市朝阳区建国门外大街22号
赛特大厦 1701 室(100004)
电话：(8610) 65123415,65155020/5021/5154/0694
传真：(8610)65155019
网址：www.btmbeijing.com
发行部：中国北京市崇文区法华南里小区 10 号楼一层(100061)
电话：(8610)67152379/82　传真：(8610)67152381
Sponsors: Information Office of Beijing Municipal Government
Beijing Tourism Administration
Producers: Beijing Foreign Cultural Exchanges Center
Beijing This Month Publications
Directors of Editorial Board: Yu Changjiang, Wang Hui, Yu Debin
Editorial Board Members: Wang Qing, Li Xuemin
Chief Editor: Liu Kaiyang
Deputy Chief-editor: Shirley Zhang
Director of Editorial Department: Sun Yougeng
English Language Consultant: Charles J. Dukes
Editors: Winnie Li, Daragh Moller, Hellen Zhou,
Photo Editor: Jiang Bo
Design & Production: Wang Xuqing, Guan Lifeng,
Xie Xinghe, Liu Jie
Director of Marketing & Sales Department: Wang Lin
Public Relations: Jenny Xu, May Fang, Fu Rong
Network Department: Leigh Finch, Michale Xiao, Sabrina Fang
Distribution: Huang Wei, Nie Tao
ISBN 7-5085-0594-8
Editorial, Sales Department: Suite 1701, SCITECH Tower, 22 Jianguomenwai Dajie, Chaoyang District, 100004,
Beijing, China
Tel: +86 10 6515 5020, 6515 5021, 6512 3415 Fax:+86 10 6515 5019
Distribution Department: Bldg. 10, Fahuananli, Tiyuguan Lu, Chongwen District, 100061, Beijing, China
Tel: +86 10 6715 2379, 6715 2382 Fax: +86 10 6715 2381
WWW: http://www.btmbeijing.com
E-mail: officialguide@btmbeijing.com

Welcome!

Beijing is a magnificent city, an exciting blend of the old and new as with some of the world's other ancient capitals, but with its own special charm and allure. Now the city is bursting with a new-found energy as it transforms itself into a modern world metropolis, while looking forward to hosting the 2008 Olympic Games.

Whether you are in China's capital city for a few hours, a few days or a lifetime, the *Beijing Official Guide* can be an indispensable aid in showing you not only the well-beaten paths of the city's must-see World Heritage List sites: the Forbidden City (Gugong), the Temple of Heaven (Tiantan), the Ming Tombs (Shisanling), the Peking Man site at Zhoukoudian (Zhoukoudian Yuanren Yizhi) or the Summer Palace (Yiheyuan) but also those attractions peculiar to Beijing that cannot be found on more conventional guides.

A thousand or more delights await visitors who wander Beijing's *hutong*, its parks and recreational areas, its lesser-known temples, famous homes, lakes and more. The *Beijing Official Guide* can help you find the "road less travelled" and enhance your visit to Beijing and China. Where are the best art galleries, Chinese dumpling shops, teahouses, Peking roast duck restaurants? Which bars do long-time foreign residents prefer? And where do those "in the know" shop when looking for special gifts to take home to friends and relatives in their home countries? The *Beijing Official Guide* has answers to all these questions and much more.

Wherever you go and whatever you do in this charming city, keep the *Beijing Official Guide* close at hand; it will deepen your experience with this historic, fast-moving political, economic and cultural centre of China.

Contents

Part A   Facts about Beijing   8

The Natural Environment . . . 8
Population 8
Administrative Districts 8
History 9
Language 10

Part B   Useful Information   13

Transport 13
Money 19
Postal Services 19
Communications 20
Visas and Passports. 21
Newspapers,
Magazines and TV 22
Bookstores 22
Photos 23
Haircutting 23
Children 23
Travel Agencies 23

Part C   Eight Areas   25

From Tian'anmen Square to
Wangfujing Street 25
Beihai, Shichahai and the Bell
and Drum Tower 26
Temple of Heaven, Hongqiao
Market and Beijing Amusement
Park 27
China World Trade Center . . 28
Workers' Stadium and
Sanlitun 28
Chaoyang Park and Laitai
Flower Market 29
798 Art Quarter and
Wangjing 30
Haidian University District,
Summer Palace
and Fragrant Hills 31

Part D   Out and About   33

Heritage Sites 33
Parks 37
Sites of Worship 40
Walks 44
Museums 45
Former Homes of
the Famous. 48

Part E   Wining and Dining   50

Food and Drink 50
Teahouses 53
Bars and Clubs 54
Chinese Style 56
Western Style 60
Asian Style 64

Part F Shopping   66

Wangfujing 66   Beijing Curio City 68
Xidan Street 66
Friendship Store 66   Golden Resources
Hongqiao Market 66   Shopping Centre 68
New Silk Market 66
Yashow Market 67   Dongdan-Dongsi 68
Panjiayuan Market 67
Liulichang 67   Shopping Centres,
Tongli 67   Supermarkets and
Gaobeidian 68   Convenience Stores...... 68

Part G Culture & Arts   70

Peking Opera 70   Porcelain.............. 71
Painting and Calligraphy .. 70   Lacquerware........... 71
Kunqu Opera 71   Architecture 72
Acrobatics 71   Traditional Chinese Medicine . 72

Part H What's On   75

Part I Mother Tongue   78

Part J 2008 Olympics   80

Green Olympics........ 80
High-tech Olympics 83
People's Olympics 84

Part K Telephone Numbers   85

Part A

Facts about Beijing

Beijing: a city that Marco Polo visited and served at the Imperial court; a city with Six World Heritage Sites, including the Great Wall and the Forbidden City; and a city where East meets West and where the past and present merge in a special way. It is no wonder that this historic capital has been chosen to host the 2008 Olympics.

The Natural Environment

Beijing covers nearly 16,808 square kilometres (sq.km.). Mountainous areas, which surround Beijing from the west to the northeast, occupy more than 10,417 sq.km of area and account for 62 percent of the city's total landmass. The remaining 6,390 sq.km area consists of flat terrain, a part of the North China or Middle Plain.

Located at 39 degrees 56 minutes north latitude and at 116 degrees 20 minutes east longitude, Beijing finds itself in a warm, temperate zone with a semi-humid climate. It has four distinctive seasons, with a short spring and autumn, and a long summer and winter. The weather in spring is usually pleasant, but it can be very dry, with occassional wild sand storms. Summer is hot and humid with an average temperature of 32 degrees Celsius (90 F) in July. Winters are very cold and dry, sometimes accompanied by windy cold fronts, with average temperatures reaching -10 C (14 F) in January.

The best season for travel is at the turn of summer and autumn, in September and October, when temperatures cool down to 15-20 C (59-68 F). In autumn, jeans and sweaters can be worn. In the warmer months, T-shirts and light trousers or shorts are the best choice.

Population

- Beijing's registered population is 14.93 million.
- Population figures include a floating or migrant-worker population that is estimated at about 4 million.
- China's 56 ethnic groups are all represented in Beijing.

The majority of the city's residents are of the Han ethnic group.

Administrative Districts

The municipality governs 16 urban districts and 2 rural counties, including Dongcheng, Xicheng, Chongwen, Xuanwu, Chaoyang, Haidian, Fengtai, Shijingshan, Mentougou, Fangshan, Changping, Shunyi, Tongzhou, Daxing, Pinggu and Huairou districts, and Miyun and Yanqing counties.

Main language:	Mandarin (*putonghua*)
Time zone:	GMT/UTC plus 8 hours
Telephone country code:	86
Telephone area code:	010
City Flowers:	Chinese rose and Florist's chrysanthemum
City Trees:	Oriental arborvitae and cypress

History

Prehistory

Beijing was half a million years in the making. Among its earliest residents were Peking man whose remains, hundreds of thousands of years old, were first excavated in Zhoukoudian in the 1920s. Along with the Sinanthropus pekinensis, or early Homo erectus, discoveries include those of a Homo sapiens (18,000-11,000 BC) people. Zhoukoudian is now a United Nations Educational, Scientific and Cultural Organization (UNESCO) World Heritage List site. Scientists from China and around the world are still probing its mysterious past.

Early Unification

According to historical records, present-day Beijing is the site of an ancient city that existed during the Warring States Period (475-221 BC). The city, Ji, rose from territorial conflict between the Ji and Yan States, and was situated north of the Guang'anmen Gate near Baiyunguan Temple.

During the Qin Dynasty (221-207 BC), the city of Ji became an administrative district. For 10 centuries, till the end of the Tang Dynasty (AD 618-907), it served as a strategic military and trade centre, and thus was constently involved in power struggles. The subsequent 200 years saw Beijing under the control of a northern minority.

852 Years as a National Capital

In 1153, Beijing was designated as China's capital by the Jin Dynasty (1115-1234), founded by the ethnic Jurchen group (who later became the Manchu) from Northeast China. The city was called Zhong Du, or Central Capital. Since then, Beijing has remained the State capital through successive dynasties except for a few decades.

Rise of An Imperial City

In 1260, as Kublai Khan (1215-1294), the grandson of the great Mongol leader, Genghis Khan, founded the Yuan Dynasty (1271-1368) in China, he built a new State capital that was to become Beijing. Dadu (Great Capital) was located further northeast than subsequent capitals. Historical records indicate that Dadu was built based on a grid plan, using a North-South central axis and chessboard layout for the entire city.

The succeeding Ming Dynasty (1368-1644) spent 15 years renovating Beijing as its capital. The size and layout of the present-day city proper was fixed during this period, as was the city's 7.8-km-long central axis, extending from Yongdingmen (Gate of Eternal Stability) in the south to the Bell and Drum Tower (Gulou) in the north.

The rulers of the Qing Dynasty (1644-1911), founded by the Manchus, added to Beijing's charm by constructing several large royal gardens in the city's northwest suburbs. These included Yuanmingyuan (Old Summer Palace) and Yiheyuan (the Summer Palace).

A City with State Protection

Since the founding of the People's Republic of China in 1949, Beijing has undergone a transformation. Nevertheless, much of the city's traditional architectural style has been preserved. The city proper, including the Forbidden City, as well as its watercourses and sites of cultural importance, has remained relatively unchanged.

Beijing is endowed with six UNESCO World Heritage List sites, 40 historical protection zones, and 3,553 other heritage sites, all under the State's protection.

Beijing's successful bid for the 2008 Olympics in 2001 has strengthened the municipality's heritage protection programme. About 120 million yuan (US$14.46 million) is scheduled to be spent on heritage protection each year between 2003 and 2008.

Language

The official language of China, known in English as Mandarin, is spoken by the largest number of people in the world. Mandarin is referred to by the Chinese as *putonghua* or "the common language," but in some regions in China, people also speak Cantonese, Shanghainese, Sichuanese or any one of a number of minority languages and dialects. Still, the vast majority of these same people share the same writing system, which is commonly called "Chinese characters." So even though a word may be pronounced differently in Hong Kong, Shanghai or Beijing in the native dialects of those cities, it's written in exactly the same way.

Chinese characters evolved over thousands of years from early pictographs to the complex and beautiful system we see today. The art of calligraphy is revered; how someone forms their writing is said to reveal much about them and their character, much as any artwork does the artist. Many old and commonly held beliefs about characters (such as allegedly being incompatible with the computer age, or all being "little drawings" of what they represent) are untrue and in fact Chinese characters show no sign of going out of fashion.

Knowledge of how to say even a few words in Mandarin will greatly increase the pleasure of any trip to China. For written Chinese, it is commonly accepted that recognition of around 3,000 of the most frequently used characters is enough to "get the gist" of a newspaper or similar publication.

BTM

BEIJING INVESTMENT GUIDE

Investment Guidance The new 2004-05 Beijing Investment Guide is loaded with useful information needed by anyone planning to do business in Beijing. Topics such as the "Selection of Industries and Sites to Invest" and "Procedures and Regulations for the Establishment of Enterprises" are included, but the Beijing Investment Guide also contains vital statistics and useful guidelines about Beijing's economic development and how you can become a part of it. The Beijing Investment Guide is sponsored by the Information Office of the Beijing Municipal Government and the Beijing Municipal Bureau of Commerce. This bilingual softbound, high-quality book is an annual publication of Beijing This Month Publications and it will help you succeed in the Beijing marketplace. Bargain priced at 150 yuan (domestic) and US$38 (overseas) plus postage.

150 RMB

北京 投资指南
Beijing Investment Guide

Useful Information

Transport

Beijing has the best, most accessible transport network in China. All levels of public transportation are readily available in the city, but driving in Beijing requires great skill, especially at road intersections, because of bicycle and pedestrian traffic. There are more than 10 million bicycles operating on Beijing's roads. Care should also be taken with taxis. It's best to use regular taxis with meters.

By Air

Beijing Capital International Airport is the largest of China's airports and is about 25 kilometres (km) or 16 miles northeast of the city centre. More than 1,000 flights arrived and departed daily in 2004.

Tips for Capital International Airport

(1) Changing money is easy at the Bank of China counter near the Arrival Hall Exit upon arrival. Use automatic money-changing machines in the baggage collection hall for quick and convenient foreign exchange; they accept most foreign notes. The rate of exchange is the same everywhere so there's no risk of being "ripped off."

(2) Never accept a ride into the city from a tout: it will be troublesome and expensive. Always take a taxi from the taxi stands for a trouble-free transfer to your hotel or office.

(3) Visit the Tourist Information Kiosk on the main arrivals floor–you can pick up the latest copy of *Business Beijing*, *Beijing This Month* or a *BTM Map of Beijing* there–and get a wide range of helpful information from the English-speaking staff.

(4) At departures, young men in bright yellow-and-pink vests may follow you. These are not touts but airport valets who provide their services at a low price. For 10 yuan, the valet will load your bags onto a trolley, guide you first to the departure tax window, then through customs and finally accompany you and your luggage to the correct check-in counter, where he will leave you ready to check-in. For business travellers, this is possibly the best *shi kuai* (10 yuan) spent in Beijing!

Customer Complaints: +86 10 6457 1666 **Air China Inquiries:** +86 10 6459 9567 **Lost and Found:** +86 10 6456 4119, 6459 8333
Medical Service: +86 10 6459 1919 **WWW:**http://www.bcia.com.cn

Airport Shuttle (16 yuan)   Tel: +86 10 6459 4375

Starting	Stops	Destination	Interval
Xidan	Sanyuan Bridge		Every 30 minutes, 6 a.m.-7:30 p.m.
Zhongguancun	Wangjing, Xiaoying	Capital Intl. Airport	Every 30 minutes, 7 a.m.-7:30 p.m.
Beijing Railway Station	Dongzhimen, Sanyuan Bridge		Every 30 minutes, 6 a.m.-7 p.m.
Gongzhufen	Anzhenli, Bei Taipingzhuang		Every 15 minutes, 6 a.m.-7:30 p.m.
Fangzhuang	Liangma Bridge, International Trade Center		Every 30 minutes, 6:30 a.m.-7 p.m.
Capital Intl. Airport	Sanyuan Bridge, Yuyang Hotel, Hotel Kunlun, Dongzhimen, Dongsi Shitiao, Chaoyangmen	International Hotel	Every 30 minutes, 6 a.m.-7 p.m.

By Train

Rail is the most commonly used transport for the Chinese to make domestic long-distance tours. There are four railway stations in Beijing: Beijing Railway Station (east Beijing), Beijing West Railway Station (southwest), Yongdingmen Station (south) and Xizhimen Station (north). Many bus routes serve these stations.

By Subway/Light Rail

Although sometimes crowded, subways and light rail are often the fastest way to get around the city area. The Beijing subway system (*ditie*) currently consists of two underground rail lines and two light-rail lines. The two most used lines, Line 1 (the east-west line) and Line 2 (the loop line), have recently been joined to the Batong Light Rail Line (extending the old eastern terminus of Sihui Dong to the new residential districts of Tongzhou District) and Line 13 that primarily serves the Wangjing and Changping areas of northern Beijing. Unbothered by the traffic on the roads, the subway can often beat a taxi across town.

It's easy to use the subway; enter a nearby station, buy a ticket at a ticket window, check your direction on a map on the platform, then ride. Use the same easy-to-use map to choose the best exit from the station. A ticket between any two stations on Lines 1 or 2 costs a flat 3 yuan. Riding between any two stations on Line 13 also costs 3 yuan and the Batong line 2 yuan. It costs 5 yuan for a ticket involving a transfer from a subway line to light-rail line 13 and 4 yuan to Tongzhou on the Batong line (or *vice versa*). Simply ask for an appropriate ticket at a ticket counter – try to tell the ticket seller where you want to go, show them a map or get a friendly local to help you. A ticket taker will tear your ticket on entry on all but Line 13, where tokens are issued that must be returned on arriving at your destinations. It's not complicated; enjoy the ride.

Transfer stations or "interchange stations" are located at Jianguomen, Fuxingmen, Dongzhimen, and Xizhimen and at Sihui and Sihuidong stations on the Line 1 and Batong lines.

Subway/light rail trains arrive every few minutes from 5:15 a.m.-10:40 p.m. Route signs are bilingual and all stations are announced on the trains in English and Chinese.

Subway lines Nos. 4, 5, 9 and 10 are under construction and will be completed before 2008. During the 2008 Olympics, 80 percent of the sport facilities will be accessible by subway.

By Taxis

There are more than 70,000 taxis in use in Beijing. Taxi starting-charge begins at 10 yuan during the day and 11 yuan from 11 p.m. until 5 a.m. The cost of a ride is 1.2 yuan (now being phased out), 1.6 yuan (most common) and 2 yuan (luxury) per kilometre, based on the quality of service. You are free to select any vehicle you wish at the taxi stand, unlike in many other countries, where you might be compelled to take the taxi at the front.

About 30,000 new, colourful, more comfortable Beijing Hyundai Sonata and Elantra models are being added to the city's taxi fleet in early 2005. Air-conditioned and capable of meeting Euro III international auto emission control standards, the new cars are a vast improvement of Beijing's taxi culture.

Taxi Survival Skills   **Hotline: 96103**

It would be very difficult to find a foreigner in Beijing who doesn't use the taxi system, so our top five survival skills for the non-Chinese speakers are:

(1) Try to know where you're going-a map or a card with your destination is ex tremely helpful to the driver.

(2) Carry small change-your driver may not be able to change a 100-yuan note.

(3) Sit in the front seat to make hand gestures more visible, being aware of the seat belt. *Zuo guai* is a left turn, *you guai* right.

(4) Say *ting xia* to stop.

(5) Ask for your receipt by saying *fa piao*.

By Bus

In Beijing, there are lots of buses and trolley buses, and also long-distance buses that travel all over China. Spacious, environmentally friendly and energy-saving buses are widely used in Beijing, and more improvements are on the way in preparation for the 2008 Beijing Games.

Generally, the buses work from 5 a.m. or 5:30 a.m. to 10 p.m. or midnight. The frequency of departure varies with different routes: usually, every five or ten minutes there should be a bus arriving at the bus stop nearest you. Buses also operate from midnight to 5 a.m. or 6 a.m. Charges vary from 1 yuan to 6 yuan depending on how far you travel.

There are four major long-distance bus stations: Dongzhimen (in the northeast at Dongzhimenwai Xiejie), Muxiyuan (in the south at Haihutun, Fengtai District), Beijiao (in the north at Deshengmenwai) and Majuan or Guangqumen (in the east at Guangqumenwai).

Tour Buses Tel: +86 10 6779 7546

Beijing has tour buses that travel between major resorts. They begin with the word 'tour' or 'Y'.

1. Departure each day for Y1 to Y2.

2. Departure on Saturdays, Sundays and holidays for Y6 to Y18.

3.The price covers one-round ticket and it does not include the ticket for the scenery.

Line	Departing time	Departure Place	Scenic spots	Price (yuan) Bus	Price (yuan) LuxuryBus
Y1	6 a.m.-noon	Qianmen	Juyongguan Section of the Great Wall,	45	50
Y1Z	(Tues., Thur., Sat.) 6:30-8 a.m.	Qilizhuang		45	50
	(Sat., Sun.) 6:30-7:30 a.m.	Wanyuanlu		45	50
Y2	6:30-10 a.m.	Beijing Railway, Libo Ximen, Great Hall, Dongzhimen	Badaling Section of the Great Wall,	45	50
Y2Z	6:30-9:30 a.m.	Chongwenmen, Xuanwumen, Hangtianqiao, Gongzhufen, Dafang Hotel		45	50
Y3	6:30-10 a.m.	Dongdaqiao, Dawangqiao	Shisanling Tombs	45	50
Y3Z	6:30-8:30 a.m.	Hepingjie Beikou, Andingmen			
	7-7:30 a.m.	Beitaipingzhuang, West of Shuangan Market, Dongsishitiao, Dianmen, Zhanlanzhongxin		45	50
Y4	6-10 a.m.	Zoo, Pingguoyuan, Yingdinglu, Xizhimen, Summer Palace, Deshengmen, Dangdai Market		45	50

Depart during weekends and holidays   Mar. 30 — Oct.15

Line	Departing time	Departure Place	Scenic spots	Price (yuan) Bus	Price (yuan) LuxuryBus
Y6	6:30-8 a.m.	Dongsishitiao, Hangtianqiao, Gongzhufen, Xuwumen, Hepingjie Beikou, Dangdai Market	Mutianyu Section of the Great Wall, Hongluo Temple, Yanqihu Lake	45	50
Y7	6:30-8 a.m.	Fuchengmen, Xuwumen, Hepingjie Beikou, Qianmen	Shihuadong Cave,	50	60
	7-8:30 a.m.	Qianmen	Tanzhe Temple,	50	60
	6:30-7:30 a.m.	Qilizhuang	Jietai Temple	50	60
	6:30-7:30 a.m.	Wanyuanlu		50	60
Y8	6:30-8 a.m.	Beijing Zoo, Pingguoyuan, Yingdinglu, Xizhimen	Longqingxia Gorge, Badaling Section of the Great Wall, Safari Park	50	60
	7-8:30 a.m.	Qianmen		50	60
	6:30-7:30 a.m.	Qilizhuang		50	60
	6:30-7:30 a.m.	Wanyuanlu		50	60
Y9	7-8 a.m.	Qianmen	Ming Emperors Wax Museum, Jiulong Amusement Park, Dingling Tomb, Juyong guan Section of the Great Wall		30
Y10	6:30-8 a.m.	Qianmen, Xuanwumen, Fuchengmen, Hepingjie Beikou	Ten Ferries, Yuju Temple	50	60
	7-8:30 a.m.	Qianmen		50	60
	6:30-7:30 am.	Qilizhuang		50	60
	6:30-7:30 a.m.	Wanyuanlu		50	60
Y11	7-8:30 a.m.	Qianmen			50
	6:30-7:30 a.m.	Qilizhuang	Yunshuidong Cave,		50
	6:30-7:30 a.m.	Wanyuanlu	Forest Park		50
Y12	6:30-8:30 a.m.	Hepingjie Beikou, Dongsishitiao, Xuanwumen, Hangtianqiao, Gongzhufen, Modern Plaza	White Dragon Pond, Simatai Great Wall	60	70
Y14	6:30-8 a.m.	Dongdaqiao, Chongwenmen, Xuanwumen	Jinhaihu Lake, Jingdong Daxiagu	50	60
Y16	6:30-8 a.m.	Chongwenmen, Xuanwumen	Hongluo Temple, Qinglongxia Gorge	43	50

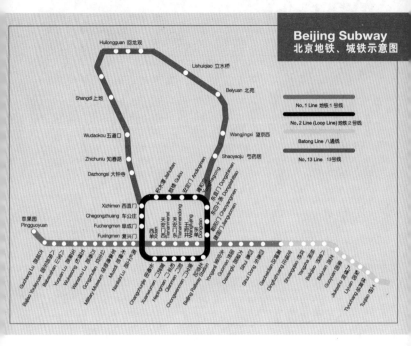

By Bicycles

China used to be called "the sea of bicycles" and in Beijing today the bicycle is still a convenient vehicle for most people. Renting a bike may be a better way to see the city at your own pace. You can rent a good bike from a hotel, paying 20-30 yuan for the day, usually requiring a deposit. You can also rent from bigger booths (for repairing bikes and pumping tires) where the charge is lower but the bikes are not as new. When you need to, put your bike in a bike park. They are easily identified by large amounts of bikes on the roadside and cost a very affordable 1 yuan.

By Pedicab

Pedicabs are three-wheeled partly-covered bicycles that are a good choice for sightseeing, especially through the hutongs, (traditional laneways) on your own. They are available everywhere and are a good value. Be warned: you should bargain with the driver first, asking how much it will cost, giving clear directions to avoid disputes. A legally registered pedicab has a certificate, and the driver should have a card hanging around his neck to notify you of it.

By Boat

Tired of traffic jams? For a change, you can travel around Beijing by boat. There are four waterway tours developed by the Beijing Municipal Government: the Changhe, Kunyuhe, Nanhu, Zhuanhe courses. In addition, there are tourist boats available in various scenic places. Feel the cool breeze in a boat, while seeing "another side" of Beijing.

Main Watercourses

Course	Departing Time	Departing Place	Destination	Price (yuan)	
				One way	Round trip
Kunyu Course (Yuyuantan Lake - Kunming Lake)	9:30 a.m.- 6:30 p.m. 10 a.m.-4 p.m.	Bayi Lake	Summer Palace	60	80
		Summer Palace	Bayi Lake		
		China Millennium Monument	Summer Palace	60	80
		Summer Palace	China Millennium Monument		
Changhe course(Beijing Exhibition Hall -Summer Palace)	9-10 a.m. 1-2 p.m.	Zizhuyuan	Summer Palace	30	–
		Beizhanmatou	Summer Palace	40	–
		Beijing Exhibition Hall	Beijing Exhibition Hall	–	70
		Zoo	Summer Palace	50	80
		Zizhuyuan	Zizhuyuan	–	60
Nanhu Course (Yuyuantan Lake-Grand View Garden)	8:30 a.m.- 4 p.m.	Yuyuantan Lake	Grand View Garden	50	–
		Yuyuantan Lake	Longtan Hu	90	–
Zhuanhe Course	8 a.m.-9 p.m.	Qihongtang Wharf	Jishuitan Pond	–	50

Other Recommended Places for Boat Tours

Shichahai /Houhai

Apart from the Hutong Tour, here, you can also enjoy boating on a long scull. Starting from the Lotus Market, passing through Yinding Bridge, the boat arrives at Houhai where local residents live. At night, you can also light up floating candles and put them on the surface of the water. Neon lights are tastefully arranged around the lake, making Shichahai even more beautiful.

Jiangnan Yuloh No. 1 (Bayi Lake Wharf – Bingjiaoyuan Wharf)

Tel: +86 10 6852 9428, 9

If you have no time to visit Jiangnan (South China), you should still not miss spending some time on a yuloh, where you can get a taste of the Jiangnan flavour. A yuloh is a traditional wooden boat widely used in southern China. While enjoying soft music, you can also have a delicious dinner on the boat.

Yuxihe River (Xibianmen – Muxidi)

Tel: +86 10 6336 1210, 6336 1310, 6336 8448

This tour provides visitors with insights into the customs of some of China's minority ethnic groups–the Miao and Dong of Guizhou Province. The tour price includes special foods such as *mijiu* (rice wine), *bobo tang* (sweets), spicy meats and other delicacies. You may enjoy your meals with the accompaniment of songs and dance.

Car Rental

If you don't want to drive in Beijing, you can rent a car and driver for a very reasonable fee. On the other hand, if you possess the necessary documents, you can rent and drive yourself. The flexible business environment of Beijing offers affordable and convenient car rentals complete with skilled and bilingual drivers. What better way to attend a punishing string of meetings around town, or to show a visiting colleague the wonders of the Great Wall?

Most reputable car rental companies offer a range of vehicles with drivers, from budget micros to luxury limousines. Be aware that not all speak English.

Business Beijing has confirmed that the following companies offer car rentals with drivers that speak English: Hertz (800 810 8883), cars with driver available; Beijing Liantuo Car Rentals (+86 10 6778 3599), cars with driver available from 400-1,200 yuan per day; Beijing Zhongyuan Car Rentals (+86 10 8448 3366) cars with driver available from 400-1,300 yuan per day. For long-term rentals with a driver, try the local English-speaking specialist, Beijing Anji Station Car Rentals, who will even buy a new vehicle if your requirements are for two years or more. You can also visit www.taxi-beijing.com for more information.

Money

Currency

The official currency of the People's Republic of China is the renminbi (RMB), which literally means "people's currency," and is also called the yuan. It is issued by People's Bank of China, the monetary authority of China.

Its basic unit is the yuan. Yuan is casually written as 元. It is formally written as 圓 to prevent counterfeiting. There are ten jiao (or mao) to one yuan, ten fen to one jiao. 100 yuan is the largest denomination. In China, prices are usually marked with ¥ in front of them and occasionally with 元 (yuan) at the end of the price.

Conversion

Subject to variation.

country	unit		yuan
Australia	AUD1	=	6.23
Canada	CAD1	=	6.84
Euro	EUR1	=	10.09
Hong Kong	HKD1	=	1.04
Japan	JPY100	=	7.38
UK	GBP1	=	14.93
US	USD1	=	8.11

Listed on: Thursday, Sept.8, 2005

Credit cards

A growing number of international ATMs can be found in branches of the Bank of China as well as in up-market hotels around the city. Major credit cards can be used in large department stores, hotels, shopping centres, and up-scale restaurants. Foreign accounts may only be accessed from foreign ATMs.

- ATMs with appropriate logos provide services for Visa, MasterCard, and others.
- Credit cards are accepted in many places, but check first.

Postal Services

Tourist hotels provide postal services. However, if you want to send important items such as antiques or cultural relics that are under customs control, you are required to consult the local branch of the international post office.

In addition to regular postal services, the International Post & Telecommunications Office handles remittances, money orders, telegraphic money transfers, international and domestic telephone and telegraph services. In the same building there is a customs office for those who need customs clearance. Additionally, packages can be collected from this office.

You can also send postcards, letters and express mail to any place in the world via China Post, FedEx or China Air Express. However, any form of publication (such as books, magazines and newspapers) or parcels, must be sent from an authorized post office.

International Post & Telecommunications Office

🌐 Jianguomen Beidajie 建国门北大街

ℹ http://www.bipto.com.cn

Communications

International calls may be made directly from hotel rooms with IDD lines. Some large post offices also provide this service. Otherwise, look for roadside kiosks with an IDD sign.

An inexpensive way to make long distance calls is by using an IP (Internet phone) card for about 4.8 yuan per minute, less than half the rate of an IDD call. IP cards can be obtained at hotels, Internet cafes and newsstands and are available both in English and Chinese.

For travellers interested in checking their e-mail accounts, all major hotels have Internet connections available in their business centres. Internet cafes can be found on the streets of the student area of Haidian District.

Business travellers in Beijing can switch to a Chinese pre-paid SIM, which saves a fortune. There are two mobile carriers servicing Beijing, China Mobile and China Unicom. China Mobile offers GSM, and China Unicom offers GSM as well as CDMA.

China Mobile

A new SIM on China Mobile (Shén Zhōu Xíng) is available from any shop with the China Mobile sign. Ask the salesperson for a pre-paid SIM with the phrase Wǒ yào mǎi Shén Zhōu Xíng SIM. You'll be shown a list of available telephone numbers. Unlike some Western countries, the SIM's price will vary based on the distinctiveness of the number. The price of a Shén Zhōu Xíng SIM starts at 50 yuan (US$12) for an average number, and rises to as much as thousands of yuan for particularly desirable numbers.

The Shén Zhōu Xíng SIM does not have any call credit when you first purchase it. You should use a "top-up card" (chōngzhí kǎ) to add value, thus allowing you to make and receive calls. The value the top-up cards carry is normally 100 yuan, although lower and higher values are sometimes available. To get on the air, simply slip the SIM into your phone – there is no PIN or password – your handset should indicate "CHINA MOBILE." It usually costs 0.6 yuan per minute for local calls. To make DDD calls, dial 12593+city code + number; to make IDD calls, dial 17951+ 0010+city code + number. China Mobile also offers an English-language operator assistance line-call 1860.

China Unicom GSM

The Unicom GSM pre-paid product is called Rú Yì Tōng ("Happy Communication"). Getting a Unicom Rú Yì Tōng SIM is as easy as with China Mobile. The basic SIM cost (without call credit) starts at 50 yuan, and the price rises depending on the number's distinctiveness. And IP card can be used on this SIM card to save money. Call 1001 (English-language operator assistance line of China Unicom) for more information.

China Unicom CDMA

If you use a CDMA handset, you're limited to China Unicom. Basic SIM and top-up card costs are the same as Unicom and China Mobile GSM, however, call charges are cheaper, at only 0.4 yuan/minute (US$0.05/minute). The process of obtaining a local CDMA number is exactly the same as in the above examples, and the English operator assistance line is the same as for Unicom GSM: 1001.

Internet/E-mail

Internet cafes are found all over the city and cost 5-15 yuan per hour.

Tips

Office Hours
In China, standard working hour are usually 8 a.m. to 5 p.m. and 9 a.m. to 6 p.m. Major malls open from 9:30 a.m. or 10 a.m. and close around 8:30 p.m. during the winter, and 9 p.m., and sometimes even later, in summer. Because traffic is bad during rush hours, tourists are advised to avoid peak-hour traffic at 7-9 a.m. and 5-7 p.m.

Electric Current
China uses a 220-volt power supply for standard domestic and business purposes. Hotels generally provide wall sockets in every room, accommodating both 'straight two-pin plugs' and 'triangular 3-pins plugs'.

Restrooms
Travellers can easily find toilets for free on the street, in office buildings, shopping centres, supermarkets, hotels and fast food restaurants.

Health
Tap water in China is considered hard and needs to be boiled before drinking. Tap water in all hotels in China is not drinkable. Inquire the staff when you check into a hotel, and they will provide either hot or cold bottled water.

Handy Phone Numbers

Area Code 区号: 010
Police Dispatch 匪警: 110
Phone Number Inquiries 查号台: 114
Time Inquiries 时间查询: 12117
Fire Dispatch 火警: 119
Medical Emergency 急救: 120, 999

Weather Broadcast 天气预报: 12121
Traffic Accident 交通事故处理: 122
Bus Inquiries 公交查询: +86 10 96166
Train Inquiries 火车查询: +86 10 5101 9999
Tourist Hotline 旅游咨询: +86 10 6513 0828

Visas and Passports

If you are coming to China for travel, you should obtain a tourist visa from a Chinese embassy or consulate in your home country. It is more convenient for tourists booked through Chinese travel agencies to get group visas for their visit to China. Tourist visas are usually good for two months, but can be extended for an extra month at the

Foreigners Section of the Public Security Bureau. A 30-day visa is activated on the date you enter China, and must be used within three months of the date of issue. These 60-90 day visas are activated on the date they are issued. Whatever you do, don't stay in the country longer than your visa allows. The fine for overstaying your welcome is 500 yuan (US$55) per day!

It is wise to carry your passport with you at all times, as you need it to register in hotels, buy plane tickets and change money. If you lose your passport, you should report immediately to your embassy, as well as the Public Security Bureau.

The Foreign Affairs Branch of the local Public Security Bureau handles visa extensions. You can also apply for a residence permit here. Extensions vary in price, depending on your nationality, for example, American travellers pay 185 yuan (US$23). Expect to wait up to five days for your visa extension to be processed. You can obtain passport photographs here (30 yuan for five, US$3.70). First time extensions of 30 days are easy to obtain and are issued on any tourist visa, but further extensions are harder to get and might give you only an extra week.

Division of Aliens and Exit-Entry Administration of the Beijing Public Security Bureau

🏠 2, Andingmen Dongdajie 安定门东大街 2 号　● 8:30 a.m.-noon, 1-4:30 p.m., Monday-Saturday　☎ +86 10 8401 5292　🌐 http://www.bjgaj.gov.cn

> **There are nine categories of visas, as follows:**
>
> **Type / Description**
>
> **L** Travel / **F** Business or student / **D** Resident / **G** Transita / **X** Long-term student / **Z** Working / **C** Flight attendant / **J-1** Foreign journalists resident in China / **J-2** Foreign journalists on brief reporting trips to China

Newspapers, Magazines and TV

Beijing offers a wide range English-language magazines and newspapers of interest to travellers, including *Beijing This Month*, *Business Beijing*, *That's Beijing*, *City Weekend*, *Time Out*, *Beijing Weekend* and *China Daily*. These are available, for free, at most four- and five-star hotels, in Sanlitun and in embassy-area bars and restaurants.

It's also easy to get issues of popular imported English-language magazines, such as *Time*, *Newsweek*, *Far Eastern Economic Review* and *The Economist* and other foreign-language publications from the bookshops of four- and five-star hotels.

Beijing's larger hotels have satellite dishes that can receive dozens of channels from all over the world, including America's CNN, NHK from Japan and Star TV from Hong Kong. CCTV-9 is an international English-language channel provided by the central government, with programmes introducing Chinese political, economic and domestic news and information about the culture, Chinese language, economy, history and daily lives of the Chinese people.

Bookstores

Gone are the days when all you could find to read in a foreign language at a local bookstore were either political tomes or "classic" novels by "dead white guys."

A recent perusal of the shelves at the Xidan Book Mansion, the Wangfujing Bookstore and the Beijing Foreign Languages Book Store revealed that the choices available to discerning book buyers are increasing, with offerings in English such as the *Harry Potter* Series, the *Great Books of the Western World*, the works of V.S. Naipaul, Anne Rice, Salman Rushdie and other contemporary writers together with the great writers of the past such as Hemingway, Faulkner, D.H. Lawrence, Balzac and others. In addition, guidebooks for foreign visitors and books on Chinese tourist sites, culture, furniture and architecture are also available at the above three bookstores and Beijing Friendship Store at Jianguomen.

The shelves containing works in other languages such as Russian, Japanese, French and German are also getting longer. Be sure to visit the Third Floor of the Beijing Foreign Languages Book Store in addition to viewing English selections on the First Floor.

Also search for "gems" in foreign languages at the book sellers' stalls at the Panjiayuan Curio or "Dirt" Market in Southeast Beijing, just inside the Third Ring Road off Panjiayuan Lu.

Photos

Photography is very popular in Beijing, and it's very easy to buy film and get it processed at stores operated by chain stores such as Kodak, Konica, Fuji and Jinglida. Print images can be digitized or prints can easily be made from digital cameras. Enlargements are easily made. For the professional, there are professional photo labs that can handle prints, slides or digital imaging. The average price for ordinary film development is 0.6 yuan, and 1 yuan for a digital photo.

Haircutting

Top quality haircuts can be found at the Silian Hair Salon on Wangfujing Avenue, a company with a history of five decades, but the prices are steep. Other excellent hair salons are found throughout the city. At these salons everything from a simple haircut to the most stylish of hair designs are available, but also head and shoulder massages, pedicures and manicures and other personal care services. About 10-30 yuan will get male travellers a haircut, shampoo and simple massage. Prices for women are somewhat higher, but are reasonable.

Children

Baby food and milk powders, domestic and imported, are widely available in supermarkets, as are the basics such as nappies, baby wipes, bottles, creams, medicine, clothing and others. Don't be surprised if a stranger picks up your child or tries to take them from your arms: Chinese people openly display their affection for children.

Travel Agencies

Beijing has abundant tourist resources. More than 200 tourist spots are open to visitors from all over the world. About 456 travel agencies operate in Beijing, employing more than 5,000 tourist guides, who speak as many as 21 foreign languages. Most hotels also offer excursions to important sites. The average cost of a city tour is 300 yuan. The following are four of the biggest travel agencies in Beijing:

China Youth Travel Service Company, Limited (CYTS)

中青旅总社

📍 F17, AVIC Building, 10B Dongsanhuan Zhonglu, Chaoyang District

朝阳区东三环中路乙 10 号艾维克大厦 17 层

☎ +86 10 800 810 0138

🌐 http://www.cytsonline.com

China Travel Service Head Office

中国旅行社总社

📍 2 Beisanhuan Donglu

北三环东路 2 号

☎ +86 10 6462 2288

🌐 http://www.ctsho.com

China International Travel Service Company, Limited

中国国际旅行社总社

📍 1 Dongdan Beidajie, Dongcheng District

东城区东单大大街 1 号国旅大厦

☎ +86 10 800 810 0177 (overseas travel), 800 810 0154 (domestic)

🌐 http://www.cits.com.cn

BTG International Travel and Tours

北京神舟国旅

📍 inside the Beijing Tourism Building, 28 Jianguomenwai Dajie, Chaoyang District

朝阳区建国门外大街 28 号北京旅游大厦内

☎ +86 10 6515 0099

🌐 http://www.btgtravel.com

Sidebar

Some lovable characteristics of Beijingers:

Humorous, passionate, friendly, optimistic, direct, talkative, proud of their history, concerned about politics and are easily satisfied

Eight Areas

From Tian'anmen Square to Wangfujing Street

Within easy reach of conveniently located central hotels and the smooth running subway Line 2, the area from **Tian'anmen Square** to **Wangfujing** is a good starting point for any sightseeing itinerary of Beijing.

While orientating yourself in the city, it is useful to imagine a series of semi-linear circles resting on a grid system and emanating outwards from the Forbidden City. This area is the natural heart of the city. Standing on **Chang'an Jie**, with your back to Tian'anmen Square and facing the **Forbidden City**, you are looking north. Chang'an Jie connects **Dabeiyao** in the east and runs to **Shijingshan**, a distance of 38 kilometres. To your left, is **Xicheng District**, and on the right, in the east, is Wangfujing.

Around Tian'anmen Square the **Gate of Heavenly Peace**, **Great Hall of The People** and **China National Museum** are all worth a visit. The body of **Chairman Mao** lies in the **Mao Zedong Mausoleum** in the southcentral part of the Square. A must for all city visitors, these important attractions usually require some waiting time.

To the east, Wangfujing is an important shopping centre and a focal point for Chinese and foreign visitors to the city. The malls at **Oriental Plaza** provide a western shopping experience that attracts huge crowds at holiday time.

The site of Imperial China over a 500-year history, the Forbidden City is breathtaking. Spread out over 720,000 square metres (sq.m.), 800 buildings and 9,999 rooms, the city will challenge any seasoned traveller to leave unimpressed. Home to Emperors of the Ming and Qing dynasties (1644-1911) the Forbidden City is also known as the Imperial Palace and Palace Museum. Constructed in the early 1400s by Emperor Yongle, the Forbidden City remained an Imperial Palace until 1924. A fire in 1644 burnt the original wooden structures to the ground and most of what stands today dates to after the 18th century.

The last Emperor Pu Yi (1906-1967) left the City in 1924. In ancient times, gongs and bells would sound around the massive **Meridian Gate**. Within, the Emperor was surrounded by a massive staff and the many concubines and members of the Imperial family. No other men were allowed in the city at night except the Emperor's eunuchs.

To get around this area, use the services of a pedicab, a semi-covered bicycle rickshaw. Usually manned by very helpful and colourful local characters, the pedicab lets you see the sights and, in the summer time, stay cool. Watch the prices though and remember, bargain!

A suggested route might be to walk the length of Wangfujing, taking in between **the Foreign Languages** and **Wangfujing bookstores** at the top and bottom of the street, not missing out on the silk and clothing shops between. Hop onto a pedicab at the top of the street and head down **Jingshan Qianjie** towards the Forbidden City. You can enter the City opposite **Jingshan Park**. Further west is **Beihai Park**, another enchanting, centrally located former Imperial Park.

Beihai, Shichahai and the Bell and Drum Tower

One of Beijing's most popular spots for young fashionable Chinese, the **Houhai Lake** area is a perfect place, day or night, to settle into a roadside cafe and watch the world go by. People come to the area to eat and a huge variety of food is available all round the lake and the nearby Beihai and Shichahai lakes. Bars provide a festive atmosphere, with music and laughter spilling over to the lakeside.

The Drum and Bell Tower at **Gulou Dongdajie** is a good starting point. The Tower was once a timepiece of the Ming Dynasty (1368-1644) that timed the beating of drums to the hours of the day. Today, it serves as a vantage point for tourists who want an unusual view of the city. Near by, on **Di'anmen Dajie** is **Yandai Xie Jie**, a narrow alleyway that connects the main street to the lakes. Filled with curiosity shops, cafes and bars, don't miss Yandai if you are in the area. The xie jie (winding street) recalls a time when the city was almost entirely composed of narrow winding streets.

To get your bearings Yandai Xie Jie (Tobacco Pipe Lane) connects **Yinding Qiao** (Silver Ingot Bridge) to the east and the Drum and Bell Tower at Gulou to the west. Yinding Qiao is a pedestrian mall and leads directly into the lake if approached on foot.

Houhai connects **Xihai** to the north, while **Qianhai** connects **Beihai,** and **Beihai Park** to the south. The bars, restaurants and cafes in the areas around Houhai and Qianhai reinvent themselves on a regular basis, but some time-honoured establishments including the **Nuage Restaurant** on the east side of Qianhai and the **Houhai Cafe and Bar** on South Houhai.

Part of the charm of the area, of course, is the lakes themselves. Usually frozen in winter, the summer months attract large numbers of boat-lovers who are content to lay back on punts or energetically manoeuvre pedal boats in the sunshine. Motor boats are also available.

Beihai Gongyuan (Beihai Park) is a stone's throw from the Houhai lake area and is worth devoting a part of a day to see. Dating from the middle of the 11th century, the park is the largest of Beijing's municipal parks and is located near the back door of the Forbidden City.

Stretched out over 86 hectares of lush gardens and woods, the park was a former playground of the Imperial families and contains many unique features peculiar to Beijing's history.

At the southern end of Beihai Park, the **Round City**, a walled, elevated landform immediately to the east of the **Great Marble Bridge**, dates from the Liao Dynasty (916–1125) and is said to be built on the site of a palace of former Mongol ruler **Kublai Khan**.

Across the bridge on Jade Islet, the sublime 36-metre-high **White Dagoba Temple** rises through the trees. Rebuilt in the 18th century, the temple commemorates a visit by the Dalai Lama in the mid-17th century. The **Xitian Fanjing Temple** to the north houses three giant statues of Buddha.

The park opens at 6 a.m. Rise with the dawn and you will catch Beijing locals dancing the waltz, making it a memorable moment to capture on film.

Temple of Heaven, Hongqiao Market and Beijing Amusement Park

The area around **Hongqiao Market**, also known to locals and ex-patriate residents of Beijing as the **"Pearl Market,"** is a lively place especially at weekends, that captures the life of the Chinese market . Called the Pearl Market because, not surprisingly, it sells a great variety of natural and cultivated pearls. The market is a place to visit on an early weekend morning. So you can get the best deal on your purchases and avoid the rush. The market has a fish and dry goods section in the basement. From the first floor up, retail goods of all kinds are available. Clothing, fashion accessories, shoes, sports clothing and music and technical equipment are available at hard-to-beat prices. Don't forget to bargain!

Across the road from Hongqiao is the majestic **Temple of Heaven**, the most visited and spectacular of Beijing's heritage sites or city parks. Indeed, it may well appear heaven-sent after a morning bargaining for special gifts for friends and family at Hongqiao.

Tiantan Gongyuan (Temple of Heaven) is now a much-used symbol of China's capital. Originally a place of Imperial worship, the park and temples are located in a 267-hectare orderly and peaceful setting.

Composed of a complex combination of round (heaven) and square (earth) elements, the park's exciting architecture and layout come to life as you experience the white marble **Round Altar**, the **Echo Wall** and **Imperial Vaults** and **Hall of Prayers for Good Harvests**.

The Echo Wall invites park visitors to enjoy some spectacular and ancient science. To the north of **the Round Altar**, the Wall carries sound round its 65-metre diameter allowing a softly spoken whisper to be heard at the opposite end. Children love it!

Dating from1420, **The Hall of Prayer for Good Harvests** has an artistic arrangement of structure and design. Gaze at the ceiling and let your eyes track the layers and weaves of colours and their composition.

The park provides visitors with many opportunities for taking a rest with fine secluded spots found on benches, in archways and under magnificent ancient trees that shade hot faces and tired feet from the scorching summersun.

If you are an early riser, experience the dancing and exercising as locals twist, twirl and stretch as the sun comes up when the park opens at 6 a.m.

The **Beijing Amusement Park** is a fun ride for any visitor new to the capital and a clear favourite for local Beijingers and their children. Family tickets ensure an action-packed outing for all. The environs of Longtan Lake in Longtan Park provide the perfect family day out around if a break is needed from the Amusement Park. Boat rides on the lake and delicious snacks to suit all tastes will keep even the wildest of young toddlers happy.

China World Trade Center

In the 1990s, the **China World Trade Center** on Jianguomenwai Dajie (east of Chang'an Jie), added to Beijing's already magnificent architectural heritage. Modelled on corporate sites from abroad, the China World in "Downtown" Guomao is now a focal point of international business and trade in the capital.

The Towers at China World house the Beijing offices of multinationals such as **Shell Oil** and **Walt Disney** and attract fashion-fanatics who shop for luxury goods. The **Shopping Malls** at China World are full of purveyors of high-end goods catering to the needs of the rich and famous, and the fashion houses of Paris, New York and Milan are all represented. While Beijing abounds with shopping malls, none are quite like this one.

From **Gucci** to **Ermenegildo Zegna** to **Dior**, the marble floors of the China World resound to the sound of well-heeled footsteps. The likes of **Starbucks** and **Häagan Daz** provide necessary refreshment for tired shopers and make interesting places for exciting rendez-vous for corporate counterparts and busy upmarket Beijingers.

In the China World complex, just above the Shopping Malls, the **China World Hotel** offers five-star accommodation with restaurants, bars and health facilities to match. Superb service and elaborate interior design make the pampered patron feel right at home. Take afternoon tea in the hotel's foyer to the accompaniment of orchestral music.

Also within in the China World complex, the **Traders Hotel** provides busy executives and corporate professionals on the go with all the support needed to make their stay in Beijing as comfortable and convenient as possible. The Garden Terrace of the Traders Hotel gives hotel guests and non-hotel patrons an opportunity to dine al fresco in a relaxing and fun environment at the heart of one of the world's busiest cities.

China World is the corporate heart of this dynamic city. Easy to get to by taxi or conveniently located subway, take an afternoon off from sightseeing and treat yourself to the welcoming, air-conditioned cool of the China World experience.

Workers' Stadium and Sanlitun

The **Sanlitun** area, a well-known stomping ground for city visitors and foreign residents far from home, is where people in the know and Beijing locals come to relax. Numerous trendy cafes and bars dot the Sanlitun landscape. Take a rest in the shade of its large trees, umbrellas and awnings during the day, then return to party in the bars and restaurants in the evening.

Surrounded by diplomatic housing and many of the official embassy residences of the foreign diplomatic community in Beijing, from **Gongti Beilu** to **Dongzhimenwai**, the Sanlitun area is a curious juxtaposition of the quiet and secluded and the upbeat downtown roar and feel of the party set. A truly international environment, Sanlitun is a dynamic and ever-changing environment that keeps the party-lovers coming back. A little full-on for more sedate tastes, Sanlitun is also known as **Jiuba Jie** or **Bar Street** by Beijing locals (worth taking note of for that taxi ride.) Look out for Bar Street favourites **Apertivo**, **Bar Blu**,

Kai Bar, and **The Tree**. Restaurants on Bar Street include Alameda, the much-acclaimed Brazilian eatery run by expert chef Gaby Alves, located behind North Bar Street.

Crossing **Dongzhimenwai**, going north, Sanlitun becomes more sedate, its leafy streets peppered with charming restaurants serving international cuisine. On North Street you can find Jenny Lou's, a Western-goods supermarket chain popular with the foreign community. This shop is owned and run by a very hard working Chinese woman of the same and name Next door there are three restaurants, side-by-side, that provide quality food and great entertainment, places you might make your local favourites while visiting the city. Another interesting fact, the restaurants are owned and run by two women from Sichuan Province.

Assaggi, **The Pagoda Tree** and **Gold Barn**, each with their unique charms, have roof gardens, sidewalk tables and lounge and bar areas. These are quality restaurants where you'd be advised to make reservations befoerhand. Assaggi is an Italian restaurant that serves its upmarket clientele in tasteful surroundings, and the food is great! The roof garden is a favourite spot to dine and cool down with the help of gentle summer breezes and shelter from sun under lush green trees.

The Pagoda Tree is an unusual theme restaurant combining Spanish-style decor and Taiwanese cuisine. Just up the street, the Gold Barn is another concept establishment with quite a few treats in store. Recreating the atmosphere of 1930s Shanghai, the Barn is spread out over three floors and is elaborately decorated with antique furniture and home furnishings.

Back on Gongti Beilu, the **Workers' Stadium,** a monument to Chinese sporting history, is an open-domed structure that also hosts various concerts.

Housing specialised sporting stores, health shops and teahouses, the Stadium grounds are also home to some fine restaurants. A staple of western dining tastes in Beijing, the **Outback Steakhouse** serves up one of the best steaks in town. With decor from Anhui and food from Sichuan, the **Le Quai Restaurant** is a firm favourite of the city's rich and famous. A terrace overlooking a small lake gives diners added incentive to make their way cross-town to see and be seen at one of the top trendy Chinese restaurant in the capital. Upstairs, the equally trendy **Beijing Art Now Gallery** (BANG) hangs cutting edge art that captures China's past and present and serves an international client list. Artists such as Chinese favourites Zhang Xiaogang, Yue Minjun and Wang Guangyi do not disappoint.

Other restaurants in the area include the artistically inspired **Green T. House**, a composite Asian-fusion restaurant and art gallery and the Mediterranean bistro at Morels. If you're in the area and fancy some late-night dancing, don't forget to check out **Vics**, **Babyface** and the **Havana Cafe**, all nightspots with a local flavour!

Chaoyang Park and Laitai Flower Market

Chaoyang Park is a relatively new addition to Beijing's municipal parks and it now includes the largest green space in the city. Neatly positioned between the Third and Fourth Ring roads, the park is a centre of entertainment and has recently become the site for great restaurants, bars and nightclubs, particularly at the West Gate.

Although the large lake within the park is frozen in winter, in summer pleasure boating dwarfs the park's many other activities. There is also a full-scale entertainment centre accessible from the park's South Gate.

The West Gate, well known to local foreign residents, is the entrance closest to the **Goose and Duck Pub**, an expatriate watering hole. Access to the Park's lakes is but a few minutes' stroll. The West Gate is next to some great restaurants including **Annie's**, a newly expanded Italian bistro, **The World of Suzie Wong**, the excellent late-night 1930s Shanghaiesque lounge bar and another Jenny Lou's supermarket outlet, popular to almost everyone who loves cheese, butter and olive oil, and other hard to find items.

Near the South Gate of Chaoyang Park, you will find **The Big Easy**, a jazz joint selling hamburgers and beer. Across the road you will find **Latinos**, a late night Latin dance bar that swings!

Around Chaoyang Park, new gilt-edge housing accommodates Beijing's most successful people. **Palm Springs**, **Park Avenue** and **Fairview Gardens** are but a few of the new apartment complexes with rooms to rent in the area.

Continue along up **Chaoyang Park West Road** and you will reach Ladies Street, also known as the **Laitai Flower Market**. New to the city, it's great for recreation, short visits or decorating a home. The flowers and other items available at Laitai will surely set the romantic side of you afire! It is a brilliant place for turning a humble home into a tropical paradise. Abundant plants and flowers, pots and shrubs, vines and miniatures trees and puppies, fish and clothes make sure you cannot leave empty handed!

Remember, go to Laitai Flower Market with things to buy in mind otherwise the amount of choices can be mind-boggling and, as always, remember to bargain. The by-word of Beijing shopping is bargain! bargain! bargain!

798 Art Quarter and Wangjing

The **798 Art Quarter** is located in **Dashanzi**, an area to the northeast of Central Beijing and now home to some of Beijing's best art galleries and most influential artists. Formerly a large State-owned enterprise built by Russia in early 1959, the old factory complex now provides a context for contemporary art to flourish in modern China.

Artists and cultural organizations began using the space in 2002 for design, photography, publishing, exhibitions, performance and art. Rented space in the factory area was converted to individual workshops, and exhibition spaces and independent studios for artists working in the fields of art, architecture, music and fashion.

The 798 Art Quarter and culture project has generated worldwide interest and should definitely not be neglected on your Beijing art tour.

Worth seeing in the Quarter: **798 Photographic Gallery**, **The Long March Space**, **Chinese Contemporary Gallery** and the **Vibes Club**, not forgetting **Cafe Vincent**.

Wangjing is packed full of things that western visitors to the city might need, should the tire of things Chinese. Near the **Lido Hotel** that houses **Starbucks**, there is a European delicatessen and several western bars and restaurants. Cafes like **Sculpting in Time** offer a fused mixture of Chinese and western cafe culture in a pleasant, relaxed environment. The food is good there too! Art areas including **Feijiacun** and **Suojiacun** are also located in this area. Avant-garde artists and their artworks are exhibited here.

Antique shops, health and recreation centres and the **Beijing United Family Hospital** are all located in close proximity in the area around the centre of Wangjing. Jewellery stores, interior design and picture framing shops are also close by.

Haidian University District, Summer Palace and Fragrant Hills

Haidian is known as the student district of Beijing but not for the usual sights that identify a university district like shabby living quarters and wild unkempt youths sprawled about in neighbourhood cafes and bars. Haidian is best known for its many university campuses, its elegantly attired young Chinese student population and its fashion-conscious, trend-setting men and women that graduate to fill the many new and emerging employment posts across China's cities. Haidian is also known for its higher-than-usual percentage of westerners who come to Beijing to teach and study in the universities of the district and also to work in the many State enterprises that employ **Foreign Experts** to assist in the development of China's transition into a socialist market economy.

Many universities are famous among the Chinese but perhaps none quite as famous as **Bei Da (Peking University)**. More than 100 years old, Bei Da has educated some of China's brightest men and women. Home to 46,000 students, Bei Da is a composite of a former US missionary school, **Yanjing University**, and **the Chinese Metropolitan University** of the former Qing Dynasty. An elegant, peaceful retreat from the hustle and bustle of Beijing daily life, the campus of Bei Da is shaded and cool in summer, frozen and tranquil in winter. The lakes around the campus provide a perfect opportunity to rest under a tree or sleep away a hot summer afternoon.

Other campuses worth taking a brief tour at in the district include **The People's University** also known as **Renmin Daxue**.

Deluxe accommodation is available at **State Guest House** on **Fuchengmenwai** that, as the name may suggest, houses VIP travellers and business guests visiting the city.

The **Summer Palace** is one of the most-visited and important sites on the Beijing tourist itinerary and with good reason. Also called the **Yiheyuan**, the palace is a large site and needs the better part of a day for it to be covered comfortably. In contrast to its original use as an Imperial retreat, the palace today is quite a busy place but don't let that put you off. Seen on a bright winter morning or dazzlingly hot summer afternoon, the palace is a memorable part of anyone's China experience. The palace is mostly a large cultivated garden containing the remains of buildings built in the 18th century that were badly damaged in an **Anglo-French Invasion** in the 1860s. **Kunming Lake** is the dominat feature with its **17-Arch Bridge** that connects **South Lake Island** to the rest of the park. The buildings that remain include the **Hall of Benevolence and Longevity** and the majestic **Long Corridor**. Further up the hillside, **Fragrance Pavilion** and the **Temple of the Sea of Wisdom** are worth the short climb. Look out for Empress Dowager Cixi's marble boat, an extravagant display of an imperial power and wealth by the ruling house. Made of marble, the boat rests in the lake water but cannot move.

Take Note: The Summer Palace (Yiheyuan) should not to be confused with the Yuanmingyuan, the Old Summer Palace, an earlier royal summer retreat that was also ransacked by British and French troops during the Opium Wars.

Fragrant Hills Park, called **Xiangshan Gongyuan** in Chinese, is just the right place for a mountain walk. Located close enough to the city centre to be accessible on a day's excursion, it is also far enough to feel immersed in the countryside. Local Chinese visit the Fragrant Hills at any given opportunity to experience the fresh air, see the colourful budding blossom trees and take exercise across the mountain range. There are temples to visit such as the **Temple of Brilliance** and hotels to stay in such as the aptly named **Fragrant Hills Hotel**, a popular local haunt.

Out and About

Beijing is an easy city to get around in. With its grid system and ring roads, Beijing Municipality is divided into 16 urban districts and 2 rural counties: Inside the Second Ring Road there are: Xicheng, Dongcheng, Chongwen and Xuanwu districts. Outside the Second Ring Road there are: Chaoyang, Fengtai, Haidian, Shijingshan, Mentougou, Fangshan, Changping, Shunyi, Tongzhou, Daxing, Pinggu and Huairou districts along with Miyun and Yanqing counties.

Heritage Sites

A globally celebrated historic and cultural city, Beijing has a more than 3,000-year history, 852 of which have been as the country's capital. It is a city rich in cultural relics and its heritage sites, the Forbidden City, Great Wall, Summer Palace, Temple of Heaven, Peking Man and Ming Tombs, are listed as some of the world's most important cultural heritage sites.

The Forbidden City 故宫

A testament to grandiosity, there are few sights in the world that will take your breath away, let alone live up to its reputation. The Forbidden City is one such place. Reading about it before you go will greatly enrich your experience and enhance your understanding of China's imperial culture.

Passing through Tian'anmen to get there, chances are you will stop in your tracks, struck by the sheer scale of the place, China's largest and best-preserved collection of ancient buildings. Home to two dynasties of emperors (Ming and Qing), and also known as the Imperial Palace, its basic layout was decided between 1406 and 1420 by Emperor Yongle and it remained an imperial palace for 500 years ending in 1924. Most of what is now seen is post-18th century construction, because a fire set by the Manchu in 1644 burnt almost all the original wooden structures to the ground.

The palace and pavilions sprawl over 720,000 square metres and contain a highly "auspicious" 9,999 rooms. The courtyards and pavilions of this historic complex of buildings need at least one full day's exploration. If lucky enough to visit it during Beijing's four seasons, you will get to see how the changing sunlight, perhaps even a snowfall, alters the character of this monument.

In ancient times, gongs and bells would sound around the massive Meridian Gate. Within, the emperor was protected by a massive number of staff, surrounded by many concubines and members of his family. At night, no other men were allowed in the city except for the emperor's eunuchs.

The last emperor, Pu Yi (1906-67), left the Forbidden City in 1924.

Originally named to reflect the inviolable sanctity of the Emperor and off limits to nearly everyone else, the Forbidden City was raided in the dying days of the Empire. Unfortunately, much of the details of those days has long been gone, leaving the city a place without a context, devoid of meaning. But a rented cassette tape, with narration by Roger Moore, will provide you with much of the information needed to fill in the gaps and probe the city's intriguing past.

🏠 4 Jingshan Qianjie, Dongcheng District ☎ +86 10 6513 1892 ⏰ 8:30 a.m.-5 p.m.

💰 60 yuan (peak season), 40 yuan (low season) 🚌 1, 2, 4, 5, 10, 20, 22, 37, 52, 54, 101, 103, 109, 124, 120, 726, 728, 802, 826, 810, 814, 846, subway

Great Wall 长城

The Great Wall of China is the Eighth Wonder of The World and a must-see for any visitor to China.

You will see its image reproduced everywhere in China, but nothing will prepare you for the thrill of seeing the Great Wall for the first time. Its serpentine twists, peaks and troughs extending to as far as the eye can see, will turn even a casual visit to a treasured memory.

Its spectacular scale remains staggering even in our technologically advanced age. Like so much of China, the Great Wall offers a glimpse into the past. If these stones could talk, what tales they might tell!

In fact there are many sections, all with a different allure and all worth seeing for very different reasons. Those who can manage only a brief visit to Beijing often make a beeline for the Badaling stretch that is only some 70 kilometres northwest of the city. Restored in 1957, it is a solid, easy-to-reach section of the Wall that includes a theatre, a museum and assorted visitor facilities.

Equally well developed is the Mutianyu section that is also well served by tourist buses; it is less than 100 km from the centre of Beijing. Also within easy reach of Beijing is the 5th century Juyongguan section that was extensively rebuilt during the Ming period.

Details for the four Walls are:

Badaling Great Wall 八达岭长城

🏠 Yanqing County 延庆区 ☎ +86 10 6912 1737 ⏰ 6 a.m.-10 p.m.

💰 45 yuan (peak season), 40 yuan (low season)

🚌 You* 1/2/3/4/5 Take the 919, 920 at Deshengmen; take long distance bus at Deshengmenwai Long Distance Bus Station (the bus departs every half hour from 7 a.m. and returns early evening.)

Mutianyu Great Wall 慕田峪长城

🏠 Mutianyucun, Huairou District 怀柔区慕田峪村 ☎ +86 10 6162 6505, 6162 6022

⏰ 7:30 a.m.-6 p.m. 💰 35 yuan 🚌 You* 6, 916

Simatai Great Wall 司马台长城

🏠 Gubeikouzhen, Miyun County 密云县司马台北口镇

☎ +86 10 6903 1051 ⏰ 8 a.m.-5 p.m. 💰 30 yuan

🚌 take You* 12 at Dongsishitiao or Xuanwumen Church

Juyongguan Great Wall 居庸关长城

🏠 Nankouzhen, Changping District 昌平区南口镇 ☎ +86 10 6977 1665

⏰ 8 a.m.-5 p.m. 💰 40 yuan (peak season), 35 yuan (low season)

🚌 You* 1/2/3/4/5, or take 345 at Deshengmen to Changping, and change to a long distance bus.

"You *" means tourist bus, "Te*" means special

Temple of Heaven 天坛

Lying south of Tian'anmen Square and the Forbidden City, the park's circular Hall of Prayer for Good Harvests has become as much of a symbol of the city as the above landmarks.

This near-perfect example of Ming architecture is set in a 267-hectare park and marked by four gates marking the four directions. Emperors came to offer sacrifices and pray for good harvests in winter.

Dating back to 1420, the Hall of Prayer for Good Harvests is the apex of the park and mounted on a three-tiered marble terrace. The four central pillars denote the seasons while the "12" symbolizes the months of the year. Look up to see the dragon, the emperor's symbol, carved into the ceiling.

Viewed from above, the temples (look for the Imperial Vault of Heaven) are round while their bases are square. The pattern is no coincidence, since it is derived from the ancient Chinese belief that heaven was round and the earth square.

And if you are interested in numbers, you will be in a numerological seventh heaven. Everything here revolves around the imperial supreme number 9. The Round Altar (Yuan Qiu) is made up of white marble, in three tiers, with the top tier believed to symbolise heaven, with 9 rings of stones, each, in turn, made up of multiples of nine.

If you are lucky enough to make a visit on a less than crowded day, check out the Echo Wall, north of the altar. It is said a whisper at one end can be clearly heard at the other end thanks to superb acoustics. Children love the experience.

📍 A1 Tiantanbei Lu, Chongwen District 崇文区天坛北路甲 1 号

☎ +86 10 6702 8866 🕐 6 a.m.-8 p.m. 💰 15 yuan (gate ticket), 35 yuan (all-inclusive ticket)

🚌 2, 6, 15, 16, 17, 20, 34, 35, 36, 43, 45, 54, 60, 106, 110, 116, 120

Summer Palace 颐和园

While understandably one of the city's most visited sites, the Summer Palace still remains a great place to escape Beijing's hustle and bustle for a day.

Another of the city's truly atmospheric spots, visitors soon get a feel for the royal garden's turbulent history while ambling around prime examples of Qing architecture and pretty Kunming Lake.

This is where residents of the Forbidden City would picnic in summer, escaping Beijing's summer heat. It's easy to understand the appeal as you stroll around its cooling water features, hills and beautiful gardens.

Kunming Lake (Kunming Hu) is the obvious centrepiece, taking up about three-quarters of the total area. This was once a popular skating area in winter and a source of ice for domestic purposes. In the poetically named Hall of Benevolence and Longevity (Ren Shou Dian), Emperors would handle affairs of state. Look out for the hardwood throne and for the bronze animals in the courtyard.

Among the scores of photo opportunities available, you will find a particularly eye-catching boat, one made of marble at the command of the Empress Dowager Cixi. Popular with photographers, too, is the 700-metre-long Long Corridor (Chang Lang).

The best view of the park is from the artificially made Longevity

Hill (Wanshou Shan) on which sits the Precious Cloud Pavilion (Baoyun Ge) and the Temple of the Sea of Wisdom (Zhihui Hai). It is a great place to rest, catch your breath and look out over the city.

Just the names of some of the attractions-Cloud Dispelling Hall, Buddhist Virtue Temple, Harmonious Interest Garden (Xiequ Yuan) – are enough to stir the imagination and send the mind travelling back in time.

A 17-arch bridge takes you to South Lake Island and competes with the Jade Belt Bridge (Yudai Qiao) for the attention of photographers looking for the perfect backdrop.

📍 Xiyuan, Haidian District 海淀区西苑 ☎ +86 10 6288 1144

🕐 6:30 a.m.-6 p.m. 💰 30 yuan (door ticket), 50 yuan (all-inclusive ticket)

🚌 330, 332, 333, 346, 394, 801, 808

Ming Tombs   十三陵

Extravagant burial chambers became the final resting places for 13 Emperors of the Ming Dynasty (1368-1644).

The importance of the tombs, an essential day trip for any serious visitor to Beijing, was fully recognized by UNESCO's World Heritage Committee and they were added to the highly prestigious World Heritage List.

The tombs are a vivid presentation of a funerary culture that for hundreds of centuries held sway across China. An impressive marble archway and 7-km road known as the Sacred Path leads to the 40-sq.km area in which the tombs are found. In times gone by, officials would have to dismount at the Great Palace Gate.

The figures lead you to the Lingxing Gate. The first of the tombs to be excavated and opened to the public was Dingling Tomb. This was home to Emperor Wanli. Records suggest that it took half a million workers six years to build the tomb according to his very specific requirements. The Ding Ling Tomb was followed by two others, the Changling Tomb, the biggest of the three, and the Zhaoling Tomb.

Wan Li is said to have given a party in the funeral chamber to celebrate its completion. No fewer than 26 treasure chests were recovered there. Some of the original funerary objects have been left on the site, while others were taken for display in Beijing and replaced with copies. Changling Tomb, the resting place of Emperor Yongle, was begun in 1409 and took 18 years to complete.

The beautiful surroundings in which the tombs are located make the area a popular day trip and a great site for a picnic.

📍 South of Tianshoushan, Changping District 昌平区天寿山南

☎ +86 10 6076 1148, 6076 1422 🕐 8:30 a.m.-5:30 p.m.

💰 Changling Tomb: 45 yuan (peak season), 30 yuan (low season) Dingling Tomb: 60 yuan (peak season), 40 yuan (low season) Zhaoling Tomb: 30 yuan (peak season), 20 yuan (low season) Sacred Path: 30 yuan (peak season), 20 yuan (low season)

🚌 You* 1/2/3/4/5

The Remains of Peking Man in Zhoukoudian 周口店猿人遗址

The remains of Peking Man in Zhoukoudian are located on Dragon Bone Hill near the town of Zhoukoudian, Fangshan District. The place became world famous after the discovery of a human skull on December 2, 1929, which Chinese anthologists called Peking Man (Sinanthropus pekinensis, or early Homo erectus). The caves where Peking Man was found were recognized as a World Heritage site by the United Nations in 1987. More discoveries of ancient humans (Homo sapiens sapiens) from 1,000-11,000 years ago were made after 1929, and research at the site continues today.

The Peking Man skull is one of the world's most important archaeological discoveries. During the War of Resistance against Japan in the 1930s, the skull mysteriously disappeared. Its whereabouts remain unknown to this day, despite repeated attempts at locating it.

Peking Man is believed to have been one of the earliest primitive men to use fire. Proof has been found in ashes and burnt animal bones found in the cave. Unearthed fossil remains in Zhoukoudian include 6 skulls, 15 jaw bones, 157 teeth and countless fragmented bones belonging to 40 individual Peking Men, constituting important materials for the study of the early biological evolution of human beings and the development of early culture. After the establishment of the People's Republic of China, Zhoukoudian became a great tourist attraction.

📍 1 Zhoukoudian Dajie, Fangshan District 房山区周口店大街1号 ☎ + 86 10 6930 1287
🕐 8:30 a.m.-5 p.m. 💰 30 yuan for adults, 15 yuan for children and the elderly
🚍 take 917 at Tianqiao to Fangshan, or take 616 at Beijing West Railway Station to Liangxiang, then change Huan 2 to Zhoukoudian

Parks

Beijing has some really beautiful places where you can spend your time in solitude either walking or resting. Here we select some of the Beijing's most well known green areas.

Beihai Park 北海公园

This very large park northwest of the Forbidden City is half water and half land. The lake was actually dug during the Jin Dynasty, (12th-13th centuries). Now any visitor can rent swan paddle boats and explore the lake and its environs. In the winter the lake is frozen and ice skates are available for rental.

Kublai Khan is the reputed original creator of the park. A lavishly decorated jade vase which was presented to him in 1265 is exhibited in the Round City just inside the southern entrance to the park.

📍 Northwest of the Forbidden City, Xicheng District 西城区故宫西北
☎ +86 10 6403 1102 🕐 6 a.m.-9:30 p.m. (peak season), 6:30 a.m.-8:30 p.m. (low season) 🚍 5, 13, 42, 101, 103, 105, 107, 109, 111, 118

Jingshan Park 景山公园

Want an extraordinary view of the city of Beijing and of the Forbidden City? On a clear day one should be able to see the western mountains as well as an all-encompassing view of the gold and vermilion Forbidden City. Jingshan Park is directly opposite the North Gate. For more than 700 years, this park served Ming and Qing dynasty emperors.

Once known as the Hall of Imperial Longevity, the Children's Palace now provides after-school activities for at least 1,000 children each day. Instructions in dancing, singing, theatre, instrumental music, painting and sports are provided.

📍 North of the Forbidden City, 44 Jingshanxi Jie, Xicheng District

西城区景山西街 44 号，故宫后门对面

☎ +86 10 6404 4071 🕐 6:30 a.m.-8 p.m. (low season), 6 a.m.-9 p.m. (peak season)

🚌 58, 101, 103, 111, 124, 812, 814, 819

Zhongshan Park 中山公园

The northern boundary of this interesting park borders the moat of the Forbidden City. During the reign of the Yongle Emperor, the Altar of Earth and Grain were located here. Emperors made twice-yearly offerings to the gods of the fields and agriculture.

Now there is also a wonderful children's play area shaded by ancient cypress trees, which is extremely popular with families.

📍 West of Tian'anmen, Dongcheng District 东城区天安门广场西侧

☎ +86 10 6605 4594 🕐 6 a.m.-9 p.m. (high season), 6 a.m.-8:30 p.m. (low season).

🚌 1,2,4,5, 9, 10, 44, 48, 52, 53, 54, 59, 66, Tian'anmen West Subway Station

Changpuhe Park 菖蒲河公园

Changpuhe is also called Waijinshuihe, a pretty, renovated river park lying to the east of the Forbidden City. It was neglected and, for a long time, lay hidden under stone slabs and warehouses.

The renovation transformed this part of Beijing into prime recreational spectacle. Beautiful flower gardens and a teeming river of goldfish are among its main attractions. There are now also courtyard-style restaurants and modern amenities.

The park is always open and is truly one of the loveliest outdoors places in Beijing.

📍 Nanchizi Dajie, Dongcheng District 东城区南池子大街

The Palace of Prince Gong 恭王府

The palace is Beijing's best-kept and biggest courtyard (*siheyuan*), it is said to be the model for Cao Xueqin's *Dream of the Red Mansions*.

📍 A 14, Liuyin Jie, Xicheng District 西城区柳荫街甲 14 号

🚌 13, 107, 111, 701, 801, 823

Ditan Park 地坛公园

Just north of the Lama Temple is Ditan Park, Temple of Earth. Built in 1530, it had a similar purpose to the Temple of Heaven. Ming and Qing emperors travelled here to make sacrifices each year on the summer solstice. Ordinary citizens were allowed on the grounds for the first time only after 1911.

📍 A 2 Di'anmenwai Dajie, Yonghegong Subway Station, Chaoyang District

朝阳区地安门外大街甲 2 号

☎ +86 10 6421 4657

🕐 6 a.m.-9 p.m. 🚌 13, 27, 104, 108, 116

Ritan Park 日坛公园

In the centre of the southern embassy area and north of the Friendship Store is Ritan Park, Temple of the Sun.

The park was originally the site of a 16th-century altar where emperors made sacrificial offerings to the sun god.

📍 6 Ritan Beilu, Chaoyang District 朝阳区日坛北路6号 ☎ +86 10 8563 5038

🕐 6 a.m.-9 p.m. 🚌 1, 4, 28, 43, 57, 120

Grand View Garden 大观园

Before visiting the Grand View Garden, a visitor should read the 18th-century classic Chinese novel A Dream of Red Mansions by Cao Xueqin. The Garden area was designed and built in the 1980's as a set for the most successful television production.

The Chinese name for the garden is Daguanyuan; it is located in Xuanwu District. The area is a quiet getaway to walk through and relive the novel. There are many paths that lead you around a lake.

📍 Nancaiyuan Jie, Xuanwu District 宣武区南菜园街 ☎ +86 10 6354 4994

🕐 8:30 a.m.-5 p.m. 🚌 19, 59, 56, 423, 112, 351

Fragrant Hills Park 香山

Fragrant Hills Park, the site of several Ming and Qing dynasty temples and villas, is located in Northwest Beijing, a little over an hour from the city centre by car.

This is a popular destination for Beijingers and visitors because of its spectacular views from its highest peak that rises nearly 2,000 feet (609.6 metres) above sea level. The peak may be reached on foot or by a chairlift. The botanical gardens, Temple of Brilliance and the Indian-styled Azure Clouds Temple are some of the sites worth visiting. Late fall, when the leaves are turning red, is a wonderful time to visit.

From the 12th to the end of the 18th centuries, the Hills were a favourite hunting retreat for emperors.

📍 At the foot of Xishan Hill, Haidian District 海淀区西山脚下

☎ +86 10 8259 0297 🕐 6 a.m.-6:30 p.m. 🚌 331, 360, 904, 737

Beijing Botanical Garden 北京植物园

The 400-hectare Beijing Botanical Garden is located at the foot of the Western Hills in Northwest Beijing. Along with a large variety of plants, the garden has Asia's largest greenhouse.

📍 Wofosi Road, Xiangshan, Haidian District 海淀区卧佛寺路

☎ +86 10 6259 1283 🕐 8 a.m.-5 p.m. 🚌 318, 333, 360

Chaoyang Park 朝阳公园

Chaoyang Park is the largest forested metropolitan park built in Beijing, offering numerous attractions and superbly maintained flower and grass areas.

📍 1 Nongzhan Nanlu, Chaoyang District 朝阳区农展南路1号

☎ +86 10 6506 5409 🕐 6:30 a.m.-8:30 p.m. 🚌 115, 302, 710, 705, 988, 976

Blue Zoo Beijing 工体富国海底世界

This zoo is best known for Beijing's first saltwater aquarium. Visitors get a great view of a diverse collection of sea creatures by walking through Asia's largest (120-metre) transparent underwater tunnel. You can see 6,000 sea creatures from all over the world.

📍 South Gate of Workers' Stadium, Chaoyang District 朝阳区工体南门

☎ +86 10 6593 5263 🕐 8 a.m.-6:30 p.m. 🚌 110, 120, 118, 403

Taoranting Park 陶然亭公园

Taoranting Park is a well established old neighbourhood park. When it was completely redesigned in 1952 excavations revealed that settlements existed as far back as the 3rd century BC. Unlike other parks that were only for the use of the Emperor and his family, this park was available to everyone. During the Qing Dynasty the Taoran Pavilion was a popular meeting place for poets and other writers.

📍 19 Taiping Jie, Xuanwu District 宣武区太平街 19 号 ☎ +86 10 6353 5704
🕐 7 a.m.-8 p.m. 🚌 20, 40, 59, 102, 122, 106, 819

Sites of Worship

China respects the freedom of religious belief. Religion is as important an aspect of life as it is anywhere else in the world and belief is recognized as an individual right.

Many religions coexist in relative harmony here, with many Chinese practicing Buddhism, Daoism, Islam, and Christianity, each respected as independent but equal.

As the capital of a country with many faiths, Beijing has a great variety of sacred sites, reflecting the five religious traditions that can be found across the country.

Confucius Temple 孔庙

Confucius (Kongzi) (551-479 BC), who also bore the names Qiu and Zhongni, is acknowledged as ancient China's greatest thinker and philosopher. Confucianism remains an important aspect of traditional Chinese culture today.

Located at the junction of Ancient Culture and Imperial College streets, the 700-year-old, 22,000 sq.m temple was a sacrificial site for emperors of the Yuan, Ming and Qing dynasties.

Visitors can view the temple's relics from the compound's grand buildings. Among them is the Jinshi Inscription Stele, artefacts relating to the Chinese Imperial Examination System, and what is known as the "13 Scriptures Stele Forest." In 1988, the temple was designated a site of historical importance under the guidlines of the National Relics Protection Unit.

📍 13 Guozijian Jie, Dongcheng District 东城区国子监街 13 号
☎ +86 10 8401 1977 🕐 8:30 a.m.-5 p.m. 💰 10 yuan (for adults), 6 yuan (for the elderly), 3 yuan (for children) 🚌 13, 18, 44, 62, 104, 108, 116, 406, 807

Temple of Emperors of Successive Dynasties in China 历代帝王庙

This temple is one of the three imperial temples (Taimiao, Confucius Temple and Emperors' Temple) in Beijing. It was an Imperial temple during the Ming and Qing dynasties, used for offering sacrifices to gods and ancestors such as Yanhuang (the mythical father of the Chinese race) and distinctive Emperors and heroes in history. It existed only in rural Beijing. The magnificent "Jingdechongsheng" Hall has the same elevation and size as the Palace of Heavenly Purity in the Forbidden City. The huge red wall before the gate is of a type seldom seen in China. The buildings such as Shenchu, Shenku, Zaishengting and Jingting were constructed according to the system of Imperial graves.

North side of Fuchengmen Nei Dajie, Xicheng District 西城区阜成门内大街路北

☎ +86 10 6616 1141 ● 9 a.m.-4:30 p.m. ✪ 20 yuan (for adults), 10 yuan (for students)

🚌 13, 101, 102, 103

Buddism

Buddhism is the dominant religious philosophy in China; it first arrived during the Han Dynasty and played a central role in Chinese culture and history.

Generally speaking, Buddhism in China can be categorized into Han, Tibetan and Southern Buddhism. Han and Tibetan Buddhism are significant subdivisions; they both preserved important Sanskrit literary works that would otherwise have been lost in Southern Buddhism.

There are numerous Buddhist temples in Beijing, including some that are celebrated.

Jietai Temple 戒台寺

During any visit to China, you will encounter tour guides with tales of ancient trees in temple courtyards. One of the finest examples must be the Jiulong Pine Tree (or Nine-Dragon Pine), found inside Jietai Temple, and said to be over 1,300 years old.

Built during the Tang Dynasty, the temple is a tree lover's delight with the main complex liberally dotted with ancient pines, many of which have their own quirky names.

South of Ma'anshan, Mentougou District 门头沟区马鞍山南 ☎ +86 10 6980 6611

● 8 a.m.-5:30 p.m. 🚌 You 7* at Qianmen or 335 at Fuchengmen or take 931 at Pingguoyuan

Yonghegong (Lama Temple) 雍和宫

Yonghegong (Lama Temple) is probably the most prominent and colourful temple in Beijing. At one time it was the official residence of Count Yin Zhen, a Chinese emperor during the Qing Dynasty (1644-1911). When he became emperor in 1723, the temple colours were transformed from green (representing Buddhism and now used by the Zen sect of Buddhism) to Imperial yellow (a colour that could only be used by the Emperor of China.).

Now a working lamasery, it has three spectacular archways and five main halls, each larger than the last and all featuring courtyards and galleries. Keep an eye out for the 18-metre high Buddha in Wanfu Pavilion.

12 Yonghe Gong Dajie, Dongcheng District 东城区雍和宫大街12号

☎ +86 10 6404 4499 ● 9 a.m.-4:30 p.m. 🚌 13, 18, 44, 62, 116, 406, 807

Yunju Temple 云居寺

The Yunju (or Cloud Dwelling) Temple that is situated in a limestone cave, south of the Shangfang Mountains, grew up around a shrine. Two bone fragments found at the site were said to belong to Siddhartha Gautama, the founder of Buddhism. More than 77,000 engraved wooden blocks containing the Chinese Tripitaka or Buddhist scriptures draw large crowds to the site.

Dashiwo County, Fangshan District 房山区大石窝镇水头村南 ☎ +86 10 6138 9612

● 8:30 a.m.-5 p.m. 🚌 You 10* from 7-8 a.m. at station 22 at Qianmen, 343 at Wanyuan

Lu, 6 at Liuliqiao or 373 at Yuquan Lu or 917 at Tianqiao and get off at Fangshan, change to a minibus to Zhangfang. *You means tourist bus

Fahai Temple 法海寺

Buddhist murals that date to the Ming Dynasty (1368-1644) can be seen at Fahai (Law of the Sea) Temple on the western fringes of the city. In meticulous detail, the murals represent the meeting of Buddhist deities.

📍 28 Moshikou, Shijingshan District 石景山区模市口 ☎ +86 10 8871 5776
🕐 9 a.m.-4:30 p.m. 🚌 337 at Changchun Jie and get off at Shijingshan station or 311 at Pingguoyuan and get off at Moshikoucun.

Sleeping Buddha Temple 卧佛寺

Located on the eastern side of the Fragrant Hills, the temple was built in the 7th century during the heyday of the Tang Dynasty (AD 618-907). It was enlarged during the Yuan Dynasty (1271-1368) to accommodate a huge bronze reclining Buddha, cast in 1320 using 25,000 kilograms of bronze.

The 5.2-metre-long Sleeping Buddha depicts Sakyamuni, a founder of Buddhism. Surrounding it the 12 sculptures illustrate the mourning of Sakyamuni's 12 disciples.

Address: Wofuosi Lu, Fragrant Hill, Haidian District 海淀区香山 Tel: +86 10 6259 1283
Opening hours: 6 a.m.-7 p.m. Buses/Subway: 318, 333, 360, 714, 737, 904, Te* 5

Tanzhe Temple 潭柘寺

This hillside temple consists of pavilions, prayer halls, courtyards and a group of pagodas dating from the Yuan, Ming and Qing dynasties.

📍 Tanzhe Mountain, Mentougou District 门头沟区潭柘山 ☎ +86 10 6086 2500
🕐 8 a.m.-5:30 p.m. 🚌 307, 326, 336 and get off at Hetan station, change to a long distance bus or 931 or minibus at Pingguoyuan

Taoism

Taoism is the only religion that actually originated in China. As with Buddhism, a philosophical, then religious, tradition, it has, with Confucianism, shaped Chinese life for more than 2,000 years.

The religion is a derivative of the philosophical ideas of Laozi, a famous philosopher. A key concept in Daoism is "the Way," that is variously interpreted as giving philosophical or religious guidance to the Chinese people. At one time, it was used as an instrument of rule, but today it survives both as a religious tradition, especially in Taiwan, and as a philosophy.

The most common representation of Daoist theology is the circular Yin Yang figure. It symbolizes the balance of opposites in existence: when equally present, all is calm; when one outweighs the other, confusion and chaos appear.

Baiyunguan (White Cloud Daoist Temple) 白云观

Baiyunguan is the largest Daoist centre in Beijing. The temple has a library of 5,485 Daoist classics and many Daoists in the temple are well versed in its philosophy. During the Spring Festival, the fair at

Baiyunguan is very popular.

📍 Baiyun Lu, Fuxingmenwai Dajie，Xicheng District　西城区复兴门外大街白云路
📞 +86 10 6346 3531 🕐 8:30 a.m.-4:30 p.m. 🚌 19, 48, 114, 708, 727

Dongyue Daoist Temple 东岳庙

This is a charming temple and an active place of worship with much to fascinate the visitor. There are halls of devotion, seasonal market stalls and plentiful totems of good fortune.

📍 141 Chaoyangmenwai Dajie, Chaoyang District
朝阳区朝阳门外大街 141 号 📞 +86 10 6551 0151, 6551 4148 🕐 8 a.m.-4:30 p.m. (Tues.-Sun.). 🚇 get off at Chaoyangmen Subway Station, and walk 600 metres to the east

Christianity

Christianity (Nestorian) arrived in China as early as the Tang Dynasty (AD 618-907). The term Christianity often denotes Protestantism, with Catholicism being considered a different religion rather than a different tradition.

Today China has respect for the freedom of religious belief and allows the independent running of religious affairs.

In history, the fortunes of Christianity have waxed and waned. As a consequence of the Opium War (1839-42), the Qing government was forced to accept terms that made Christianity legal in China.

After the founding of People's Republic of China in 1949, Christianity gradually removed its foreign tag and became an acceptable and independent Chinese institution. Today it has a firm root in contemporary Chinese culture.

Islam

Islam is a religion with more than 1,400 million believers worldwide and has prospered throughout history in Africa, the Middle East, Central Asia and Indonesia. Islam arrived in China during the Tang and Song dynasties (618 BC-AD 1279) through trade links.

From the Yuan Dynasty (1271-1368), Islam became an independent religion in China, and many of its followers came from ethnic groups in Xinjiang Province.

There are now more than 100 million Chinese Muslims, many living in the deserts of Xiangchan and the more fertile regions of mid and eastern China. There are more than 40 mosques in Beijing that are open to the public.

Niu Jie Mosque 牛街礼拜寺

Niu Jie, or Ox Street Mosque, is the oldest mosque in Beijing and enjoys great reputation among Muslims of all persuasions and nationalities. It is a striking mosque and definitely worth a visit. According to legend, an ancient imam lives in the catacombs beneath the mosque and if non-believers should attempt to enter its prayer hall, he will suddenly appear and send the "heretic to Allah" by throwing small steel darts at the infidel!

📍 88 Niu Jie, Xuanwu District 宣武区牛街 88 号 📞 +86 10 6353 2564
🕐 5:10 a.m.-8 p.m. 🚌 6, 10, 50, 53, 61, 109

Chongwenmen Protestant Church 崇文门教堂

📍 D2 Hougou Hutong, Chongwen District (in the *hutong* beside Tongren Hospital)

崇文区内后沟胡同丁2号，同仁医院东侧

☎ +86 10 6513 3549, 6522 9984

🕐 7 a.m.-8:30 p.m.

Church of the Immaculate Conception (Nantang and Xuanwumentang)宣武门教堂

📍 141 Qianmenxi Dajie, Xuanwu District

宣武区前门西大街141号

☎ +86 10 6603 7139

🕐 6 a.m.-9 a.m. (3 hours for each day)

Zhushikou Protestant Church 珠市口教堂

📍 129 Qianmennan Dajie, Chongwen District (at the Liangguang Dajie and Qianmen Dajie crossroads)

崇文区前门南大街129号（两广大街和前门大街交叉口）

☎ +86 10 6301 6678

Kuanjie Protestant Church 宽街教堂

📍 51 Di'anmendong Dajie, Dongcheng District (at the Di'anmendong Dajie and Kuanjie crossroads)

东城区地安门东大街51号（地安门东大街和宽街交叉口）

☎ +86 10 8403 9432

Church of St. Joseph (Dongtang and Wangfujingtang) 王府井教堂

📍 74 Wangfujing Dajie, Dongcheng District

东城区王府井大街74号

☎ +86 10 6524 0634

🕐 5 a.m.-11 a.m.

Church of Our Saviour (Beitang and Xishikutang) 西什库教堂

📍 33 Xishiku, Xicheng District

西城区西什库33号

☎ +86 10 6617 5198

Dongsi Mosque 东四清真寺

Built in 1447 during the Ming Dynasty (1368-1644), it combines Chinese and Arabic styles like the Niujie Mosque. The mosque's library houses valuable manuscripts of the Koran, the Hadith, Islamic law and other works of Islamic philosophy, history and literature published in Egypt, India, Turkey and Pakistan. Three services are held at dawn, 1 p.m. and 4 p.m. daily. The site is also the Headquarters of the Beijing branch of China Islamism Association.

📍 13 Dongsi Nandajie, Dongcheng District 东城区东四南大街13号 ☎ +86 10 6525 7824

🕐 8 a.m.-5 p.m. 🚌 106, 108, 110, 116

Walks
Hutongs

The word *hutong* originates from the word "hottog" which means "well" in Mongolian. There are about 3,000 Beijing *hutongs*, including Nanluogu Xiang at Jiaodaokou at Beijing's Dongcheng District and hutongs around Xicheng's Shichahai area. The Qianshi Hutong has the city's narrowest passages at 44 cm. The oldest hutong is at Sanmiaojie, which was also known as Tanzhou Street during the Liao Dynasty (916-1125). Courtyards (*siheyuan*) with doors in different colours, sizes and patterns indicate the classes of the families.

Xie Jies are the interconnecting, winding streets that characterise old Beijing. These often lead into or out of hutong, the old laneways and buildings that are fast being replaced by modern housing.

Beijing Underground City
北京地下城

Completed in 1979, the city was designed as the answer to natural or human catastrophe.

🚇 62 Damochang hutong (east of Qianmen Dajie and south of Taijichang) Dongcheng District ● 8:30 a.m.-6 p.m. ☎ +86 10 6702 2657 💰 20 yuan

Red Building 北大红楼

As the former site of Peking University and the birthplace of "May 4th Movement," the Red Building started many people on their paths to fame. Some famous alumni include Mao Zedong, Lu Xun and Guo Muoruo. This four-storied building in an "I" pattern was built in 1918. It was called "Red Building" because of its red colour. It reopened to the public on July 10, 2005, as the May 4th Movement Memorial Hall.

🚇 29 Wusi Dajie, Shatan, Dongcheng District ● 8:30 a.m. -4:30 p.m.
☎ +86 10 6402 0957 💰 5 yuan

798 Art Area 大山子艺术区

The 798 Art Area is located in Dashanzi, an area northeast of Central Beijing. It was formerly a large State-owned enterprise built by the Russians in early 1959 as part of a war-reparations deal with Germany.

In 2002, artists and cultural organizations began using the space for design, photography, publishing, exhibitions, performance and art. They rented space in the factory and converted individual workshops into independent studios for art, architecture, music and fashion.

The 798 Art Area and culture project has generated great interest and should not be left out of any Beijing art tour. 798 Space, Knightland Ltd, Yan Club, Sit, Beijing Tokyo Art Projects (B.T.A.P), 798 Photo Gallery and Vibes are studios worth visiting.

Marco Polo Bridge 卢沟桥

The real name of the Marco Polo Bridge is Reed Ditch Bridge. The bridge derives from the Venetian traveller's description in his famous travelog. It was built in the early 12th century, over the Yongding River, to provide access to the capital 16 kilometres away. It is famed for its parapets that line each side, with 140 columns crowned by countless lions-as the local saying goes (if you count them there are 485.)

The bridge also bears historical significance, because this is where China's War of Resistance against Japanese Aggression (1937-45) violently began. To the east of the bridge is Wanping County and its Chinese People's Anti-Japanese Aggression War Memorial Hall and other historical sites.

🚌 take 309 at Changchunjie, or 339 at Liuliqiao

Museums

There are 121 registered museums in Beijing, public and private. Browsing cultural relics and modern exhibits in cool rooms can be an attraction during the warmer months for visitors. There are several must-see museums.

China National Museum 国家博物馆

The Museum of Chinese History and the Museum of Chinese Revolution are housed in the same building complex, which stretches for more than 300 metres north and south along the east side of Tian'anmen Square.

It has more than 610,000 relics dating to thousands of years ago. From military relics to cultural relics, visitors can get a sense of the rich culture of a historic nation. They can also get an introduction to China's modern history from the Opium War to the founding of the People's Republic of China in 1949. English translations are available for all.

📍 Tian'anmen Square (east side), Chaoyang District 朝阳区天安门广场东

☎ +86 10 6512 8967, 01 🕐 8 a.m.-6 p.m. (peak season), 9 a.m.-4 p.m. (low season)

Chairman Mao's Mausoleum 毛主席纪念堂

Chairman Mao Zedong (1893-1976), former Chinese leader and national icon, is on display. Pay homage and buy flowers for 1 yuan.

📍 11 Qianmennan Dajie, southern Tian'anmen Square, Chongwen District

天安门广场南，崇文区前门大街 11 号 ☎ +86 10 6513 2277, ext. 80 🕐 8:30-11:30 a.m. (Tues.-Sun.), 2-4 p.m. (Tues.-Thu.), (closed Mon.) 🚌 Special Route No. 1 (Te1*), 1, 2, 4, 5, 10, 20, 22, 37, 52, 54, 120, 726, 728, 802, 826, subway (Qianmen station)

Capital Museum 首都博物馆

The Capital Museum houses nearly 200,000 valuable artefacts, unearthed in the Beijing area. Among the treasures are: ancient coins, stoneware, bronzes, steles, jade, calligraphy and paintings. At the core of the collection are 800 historical relics that tell the history of the Beijing area.

Now located inside the Confucius Temple (Kongzi Miao) near the Yonghegong (Lama Temple) on the North Second Ring Road at Yonghegong Dajie, a new building housing the museum will be completed by the end of 2005 at the western end of Chang'an Jie (Avenue). Basic information about the museum and its exhibits can be accessed on computers installed there.

📍 In the Confucius Temple, 13, Guozijian Jie, Dongcheng District 东城区国子监街 13 号

☎ +86 10 6401 2118 🕐 8:30 a.m.-5 p.m. 🚌 807, 116, (Yonghegong station)

Beijing Urban Planning Museum 北京市规划展览馆

The Beijing Urban Planning Museum exhibits stunning scale models of Beijing's city planning including its business districts, Olympic Village and on the third floor the entire city of Beijing in miniature and aerial photographs. Look for your own neighbourhood – it's remarkable!

📍 east of Beijing Railway Station, Qianmen Dongdajie, Dongcheng District 东城区前门东

大街老北京火车站东侧 ☎ +86 10 6702 4505, 59 🕐 9 a.m.-5 p.m. (closed Mon.)

🚌 5, 9, 20, 44, 120, 819, (Qianmen station)

Beijing Planetarium 北京天文馆

Just opposite the Beijing Zoo in Haidian, the newly renovated Planetarium is a fun outing particularly for amateur astronomers and children. With some of the latest high-tech equipment in the field, and displaying some of the oldest examples of scientific activity in China, the new Planetarium opened late 2004.

Resting alongside an original Planetarium that was established in 1957, the 300 million yuan (US$36 million), 20,000-square-metre new Planetarium complex has three theatres, two observatories and a solar exhibition hall. The solar system exhibition hall and a galaxy exhibition hall have been the most popular since they opened. Visitors are treated to a state-of-the-art, 45-minute, mesmerising trip through the stars via the Planetarium's newly opened SGI(R) Digital Space Theatre where visitors can – for the first time – view an impressive array of high-contrast colour images including more than 37,000 stars, 30,000 galaxies, constellations, nebulae, planets, spacecraft, and deep space objects.

🏛 38 Xizhimenwai Dajie, Haidian District 海淀区西直门外大街 38 号 ☎ +86 10 6831 2517
🕐 9 a.m.-4 p.m. (Sat.), 10 a.m.-4 p.m. (Wed.-Fri.)

China National Science and Technology Museum 中国科技馆

🏛 1 Beisanhuan Zhonglu, Xicheng District 西城区北三环中路 1 号 ☎ +86 10 6237 1177
🕐 9 a.m.-4:30 p.m. (closed on Mon.) 🚌 21, 300, 302, 367, 387, 407, 718, 801, 101, 104, 201, 380, 406, 409, 819, 925, Te* 2, Te* 8

Ancient Observatory 北京古观象台

Built in 1442, the observatory is made up of eight astronomical devices designed by Jesuit astronomers and presented to the Imperial court.

🏛 2 Dongbiaobei Hutong, Jianguomen Subway Station, Dongcheng District
东城区东裱褙胡同 2 号，建国门地铁站旁 ☎ +86 10 6512 8923
🕐 9 a.m.-4:30 p.m. 🚌 1, 4, 52, 403, (Jianguomen station)

Military Museum of the Chinese People's Revolution 中国人民军事革命博物馆

The museum is composed of two four-storey wings and a main building of seven stories topped with the gilded emblem of the Chinese People's Liberation Army. More than 5,000 years of Chinese military history are on display.

🏛 9 Fuxing Lu, Haidian District 海淀区复兴路 9 号 ☎ + 86 10 6686 6114 🕐 8a.m.-5 p.m.
🚌 1, 4, 21, 337, (Military Museum station)

The China Millennium Monument 中华世纪坛

🏛 A9 Fuxing Lu, Haidian District 海淀区复兴路甲 9 号 ☎ +86 10 6857 3281
🕐 8 a.m.-5 p.m. 🚌 1, 4, 21, 52, 320, 337, 728, (Military Museum station)

Beijing Art Museum 北京艺术博物馆

The permanent collection of the Beijing Art Museum includes bronze and jade artefacts from the Shang and Zhou dynasties (17th-3rd centuries BC), and ceramics, enamels, carved lacquerware, ivory, weavings and embroideries from the Ming and Qing dynasties. Ancient coins from China and Japan complement the collection. More than 50,000 artefacts from the Neolithic Period to modern times make up the entire collection.

Ⓦ Wanshou Temple, Suzhou Jie, Haidian District 海淀区苏州街万寿寺
☎ +86 10 6841 3380 🕙 9 a.m.-4 p.m. 🚌 300, 323, 374, 811

Beijing Museum of Natural History 北京自然博物馆

The largest of its kind in China, the Beijing Museum of Natural History is located on the western edge of the Temple of Heaven. The first floor displays China's zoological history; on the second floor a study of human anatomy with human cadavers and preserved organs are displayed. The museum traces the evolution and development of human beings over the last 300-400 million years.

Ⓦ 126 Tianqiaonan Dajie, Chongwen District 崇文区天桥南大街 126 号
☎ +86 10 6702 4431 🕙 8:30 a.m.-5 p.m. 🚌 2, 6, 15, 17, 20, 25, 35, 36, 45, 53, 110, 120

China Red Sandalwood Museum 中国紫檀博物馆

Arguably China's largest private museum, most of the exhibits on display at the China Red Sandalwood Museum are not surprisingly made of red sandalwood. The museum also devotes some space to rare woods including ebony and huali (*Onmosia henryi*).

Ⓦ 23 Jianguo Road, Chaoyang District 朝阳区建国路23号 ☎ +86 10 8575 2818
🕙 9 a.m.-5 p.m. 🚌 312, 363, 718, (Sihuidong station)

Former Homes of the Famous

Former Residence of Soong Qingling 宋庆龄故居

With her sisters, Soong Qingling, a former Honorary Chairman of the People's Republic of China, was one of the first Chinese women educated in the West. She was an advocate of women's rights even before marrying the late Dr. Sun Yat-sen and becoming China's first "first lady." She was very active in national politics and in the women's movement before and after the founding of the People's Republic of China in 1949. Her belief – that women's liberation must be part of the Chinese revolution-along with the creation of the All-China Women's Federation in 1949, helped to shape the policies of China pertaining to women. Her former home has many of her personal items and effects on display.

Ⓦ 46 Houhai Bei'an, Xicheng District 西城区后海北岸 46 号
☎ +86 10 6404 4205, ext. 815 🕙 9 a.m.-5 p.m. 💲 20 yuan 🚌 5, 27, 44, 55

Former Residence of Lao She 老舍故居

As the author of the famed Rickshaw Boy, Tea House and Four Generations Under One Roof, Lao She (the nom de plume of Shu Qingchun, 1899-1966) is one of China's most beloved and respected writers. Lao She's house is fascinating for fans of his touching work.

Ⓦ 19 Fengfu Hutong, Dengshikou Xijie,Dongcheng District 东城区灯市口西街丰富胡同 19号
☎ +86 10 6514 2612 🕙 8:30 a.m.-5 p.m. 💲 10 yuan
🚌 60, 103, 104, 108, get off at the Dengshixikou bus stop

Former Residence of Mao Dun 茅盾故居

Mao Dun, the nom de plume of writer Shen Yanbing (he also used the name Dehong), was active in the famous May 4th Movement, the founder of the Literary Study Society in 1920 and was a promoter of literary realism in China. After the founding of the People's Republic of China, he served as a minister in the Ministry of Central Culture, vice-chairman of the country's Political and Consultative Committee. He also served as vice-chairman of the China Culture League and chairman of the China Writers Association for long time. The house is situated in a truly historic hutong.

13 Hou Yuan'ensi Hutong, Jiaodaokou, Dongcheng District 东城区交道口后圆恩寺胡同 13 号 ☎ +86 10 6404 0520 ● 9 a.m.-5 p.m. ⑤ 5 yuan ⊕ 13, 101, 102, 103

Former Residence of Guo Moruo 郭沫若故居

Guo Moruo is one of China's most prominent writer-poets. He was awarded many prestigious honours including the Stalin Peace Prize in 1951. His former house and gardens are immaculately preserved.

18 Qianhai Xijie, Xicheng District 西城区前海西街 18 号 ☎ +86 10 6612 5392, 6666 4681 ● 9 a.m.-4:30 p.m. (closed on Mon.) ⑤ 10 yuan ⊕ 13, 107, 111, 118, 701, 810, 823

Former Residence of Lu Xun 鲁迅故居

Lu Xun (1881-1936), father of modern Chinese literature, wrote many of his essays and novels in this small courtyard garden.

19 Ertiao, Gongmenkou, Fuchengmennei Dajie, Xicheng District 西城区阜成门内大街宫门口二条 19 号 ☎ +86 10 6616 4168 ● 9 a.m.-4 p.m. (closed Mon.) ⑤ 5 yuan ⊕ 13, 101, 102, 103

Former Residence of Mei Lanfang 梅兰芳故居

Most of the 30,000 relics belonging to Mei Lanfang (1894-1961), a Peking Opera master, on display are genuine including miscellaneous historic materials, photographs, art and international cultural exchange documents.

9 Huguosi Jie, Xicheng District 西城区护国寺街 9 号 ☎ +86 10 6618 3598 ● 9 a.m.-4 p.m. (closed Mon.) ⑤ 10 yuan ⊕ 13, 22, 38, 47, 107, 111, 409, 709, 726, 806, 810

Wining and Dining

Food and Drink

What a treat lies in store for food connoisseurs, there's so much to choose from. Listed here are some of the many cuisines available in the city.

Peking Duck

Essential to your Beijing dining experience is a brief tour of the many establishments offering Peking Duck: a delicious, lightly-smoked, rich meal complimented by pancakes, dipping sauce, vegetable filling and irresistible slivers of juicy meat, fat and crispy skin. Said to originate from Inner Mongolia, Peking Duck was first served in a Peking (Beijing) restaurant in 1855. The original recipe includes a description of how to build and fire an oven for smoking the bird!

The Quanjude Roast Duck Restaurant leads the popular duck front, and you'll find many of them in Beijing. Bianyifang Restaurant features another way of roasting duck that is also delicious.

A taste of Peking Duck is every bit as important as a visit to Tian'anmen Square.

Royal Cuisine (*Gong Ting Cai*)

As the name suggests, Royal Cuisine is composed of the recipes and dishes of the Imperial kitchens, dating from the time of the Qing Dynasty (1644-1911).

Originating from the regional cooking of the Manchu and Han people the cuisine pays as much attention to the quality of its ingredients as to its design. Dishes that have survived retain much of the culinary art of the royal kitchens and the best known are Tanjia and Honglou dishes, both lightly-flavoured and exquisite.

The Man-Han Quan Xi, a feast of complete Manchu-Han courses, was originally designed as a court banquet for the Manchu and Han people. It included at least 108 dishes that had to be eaten over three days.

Imperial Cuisine (*Guan Fu*)

Old Beijing had many high-ranking officials demanding regional homemade cooking to be served in the Imperial courts. The result is that regional recipies were all collected in the capital and so survived much historical tumult. The cuisine favours natural ingredients, exquisite condiments, long cooking times and intricate cooking utensils.

Tanjia Restaurant is the best example of Beijing's Imperial Cuisine and provides a combination of Cantonese and Beijing cuisine featuring seafood. After the founding of the Republic, Premier Zhou Enlai asked that the restaurant move to the Beijing Hotel, the best hotel in China at that time. Imperial Cuisine is still available there today on the seventh floor of Building C of the hotel.

Hotpot

When autumn hits Beijing and the weather cools, hotpot is a firm favourite.

With essentially two kinds of hotpot restaurant in Beijing, Mongolian and Sichuan styles dominate, the staple of both being mutton.

Sichuan hotpot is sicy whereas Mongolia hotpot tends to rely on a clear soup and dipping sauces, such as sesame. Many restauarnts offer a split pot. Half for those that like spice, half for those who divides into half-spicy, half-not while the Mongolian hotpot is not spicy. Standard ingredients inclued beef and chicken besides the staple mutton. Vegetables, fungus and various kinds of dofu are also popular. The pot itself is taditionally made of brass, with a central column that holds hot charcol that boils the stock. Once boiling, the stock is used to quickly cook a range of ingredients. After a few seconds the meat and vegetables are ready to eat and dipped in a smooth sesame butter sauce that is delicious and incredibly filling! Sichuan hotpot can be very spicy but also always delicious.

Snacks

All over China, snack food from the street-side is tasty and filling. Some caution may be required for the uninitiated but in general, eating where everyone else is eating is a good rule of thumb. You can have steamed bread with bean filling; flour pancakes cooked with egg, coriander, chilli, and black onion seeds; pancakes stuffed with pork, egg and vegetables. These gems can be bought from little glass cabinet's on the back of three-wheeled bicycles or from stands on street corners, hidden down leafy *hutongs*.

Regional Cuisines

Beijing is a culinary mirror held up to the four main geographic divisions that divide Chinese cuisine: South China's Canton, North China's Peking and Shanghai to the East and Sichuan to the West.

Rich in natural resources and neighbouring the sea, Cantonese cuisine is dominated by a smorgas board of seafood and the produce of a semi-tropical climate. Shanghai cuisine has much of the extremes that the city herself experiences: sharp contrasts in the weather is reflected in the variety of local flavours; the crab soup is rich and complex, the pork knuckle and red-cooked lamb also offering rginal twists on a familar recipe. Sichuan cuisine is very popular in China and has been so since the Ming Dynasty. Composed of regional variations from Chengdu, Chongqing and Zigong, it is known for having over 50 different cooking methods. Temple vegetarian dishes are also a feature.

World Cuisine

Visitors to Beijing wanting Western food will be able to find it, even if the quality is not always what's hoped for. Mediterranean food is plentiful, as is food from the rest of Europe and the US. Restaurants that immediately spring to mind are Steak n Eggs (US), Grandmas (US), Annie's (Italian) and Nuage (French/Vietnamese), all established names on the city's World Cuisine circuit.

Dining in luxurious, traditional Chinese courtyards is a fashionanble way to while away an evening for both locals and visitors.

Courtyard restaurants

Royal Palace 皇城食府

📍 Inside Changpuhe Park, east of the Forbidden City, Dongcheng District
东城区菖蒲河公园内

☎ +86 10 8511 5372

Tianqu Garden 天趣园

📍 Inside Changpuhe Park, Dongcheng District
东城区菖蒲河公园

☎ +86 10 8511 5142

Tian and Di Restaurant
天地一家食府

📍 140 Nanchizi Dajie, Dongcheng District
东城区南池子大街 140 号

☎ +86 10 8511 5557

La Cité French Restaurant
紫禁阁西餐厅

📍 115 Nanchizi Dajie, Dongcheng District
东城区南池子大街 115 号

☎ +86 10 8511 5142

Lu Ying Fang Ting Club
绿荫芳庭会所

📍 Inside Changpuhe Park, Dongcheng District
东城区菖蒲河公园

☎ +86 10 8511 5372

Gegefu Restaurant
砚逸善斋(格格府)餐馆

📍 9 Daqudeng Hutong, Dongcheng District
东城区大取灯胡同 9 号

☎ +86 10 6407 8001

Cuihualou Restaurant
萃华楼饭庄

📍 6 Lianzi Hutong, Dongcheng District
东城区帘子胡同 6 号

☎ +86 10 8404 3851

Guigongfu 桂公府

📍 11 Fangjiayuan Hutong, east from Chaoyangmen Nanxiaojie, Dongcheng District
东城区方家胡同 11 号

☎ +86 10 6512 7667

Han Zhen Yuan 涵珍园

📍 20 Qinlao Hutong, Dongcheng District
东城区秦老胡同 20 号

☎ +86 10 8402 2324

Hua Jia Yi Yuan 花家怡园

📍 235 Dongzhimen Nei Dajie, Dongcheng District
东直门内大街 235 号

☎ +86 10 6405 1908

Yuefu Restaurant 乐府酒楼

📍 218 Dongzhimen Nei Dajie, Dongcheng District
东直门内大街 218 号

☎ +86 10 8403 9067

Qian Hou Yuan 乾厚苑

📍 2 Nanwanzi Hutong, Nanheyan Dajie, Dongcheng District
东城区南河沿大街南湾子胡同 2 号

☎ +86 10 6514 0901

Zi Jing Shi Kuo 紫京食阔餐厅

📍 118 Yanyue Hutong, Dongcheng District
东城区演乐胡同 118 号

☎ +86 10 6512 3258

Noble Club 北京乙十六号商务会所

📍 B 16, Hepingli Zhongjie, Dongcheng District
东城区和平里中街乙 16 号

☎ +86 10 6428 1188

Red Capital Club 北京新红资

📍 66 Dongsi Jiutiao, Dongcheng District
东城区东四九条 66 号

☎ +86 10 6402 7150/1/2

Lijia Cuisine 厉家菜

📍 11 Yangfang Hutong, Deshengmen Dajie, Xicheng District
西城区德胜门大街羊坊胡同 11 号

☎ +86 10 6618 0107

Tanyuan Imperial Cuisine
谭园官家宴

📍 10 Huguosi, Xicheng District
西城区护国寺 10 号院
Tel: +86 10 6617 7098

Meijia Cuisine 梅府家宴

📍 24 Daxiangfeng Hutong, Xicheng District
西城区大翔凤胡同 24 号

☎ + 86 10 6612 6845

Teahouses

Tea is integral to contemporary Chinese society and a mainstay of economic and cultural activity that has not wained since the days of old Beijing. In those days, teahouses were the centre of social activity and populated with the chatter of people from all walks of life. In these teahouses noblemen, Imperial officials, touts and peddlers chose their tea carefully and caught up on the day. Today, teahouses in China still have the same function but with not quite so much bustle, having adopted some of the aspects of peace and contemplation associated with Japanese tea culture.

Experience traditional Chinese teahouse culture and tea ceremonies. Become a discerning tea drinker.

Tips

- Beijing Restaurants usually do not require tipping or service charge. Some more expensive restaurants will charge 15 percent service.
- Opening times usually 11 a.m.-2 p.m. and 5 p.m.-10 p.m.
- Menus may not have been written in English, so be warned: bring a friendly translator!!
- Do not worry about getting the chopsticks right first time: practice not perfection!! Do observe some of the taboos associated with eating in China.

Lao She Teahouse 老舍茶馆
- Bldg 3, Zhengyang Shichang, Qianmenxi Dajie, Xuanwu District
  宣武区前门西大街正阳市场 3 号楼
- +86 10 6303 6830

Cha Jia Fu Teahouse 茶家傅
- Inside Houhai Park, Deshengmen Nei Dajie, Xicheng District
  西城区什刹海公园内
- +86 10 6616 0725

Ming Sheng Xuan 茗圣轩茶艺馆
- Building 3, Yuyou Hutong, Ping'an Dajie, Xicheng District
  西城区平安大街育幼胡同 3 号楼
- +86 10 6618 5528

Jingzhiyu Teahouse 静之隅茶艺馆
- West Gate of Chaoyang Park, Chaoyang District
  朝阳区朝阳公园西门
- +86 10 6591 0505

Ming Hui Cha Yuan 明慧茶苑
- Dajue Temple, Bei'anhe, Haidian District
  海淀区北安河大觉寺
- +86 10 6246 1568, 6246 1569

Ke Zhong Zuo Cha Guan 客中作茶馆
- 1/F, Guanghuaxinju Guanghua Lu, Chaoyang District
  朝阳区光华路光华欣居首层
- +86 10 6583 0451

Ning Sheng Xuan Teahouse 宁盛轩茶艺苑
- 1/F, East Building, B15, Wanshou Lu, Haidian District
  海淀区万寿路乙 15 号南院东 1 楼
- +86 10 6825 0870

Tianqiao Happy Teahouse 天桥乐茶园
- 113 Tianqiao Market, Beiwei Lu, Xuanwu District
  宣武区北纬路天桥市场 113 号
- +86 10 6304 0617

The EatTea Teahouse 留贤馆
- 28, Guozijian Jie, Andingmenwai Dajie, Dongcheng District
  东城区安定门外国子监街 28 号
- +86 10 8404 8539

Qiao Ying Teahouse 桥影茶坊
- North of No.6 Apartment, Guanghua Xili, Chaoyang District (North to Guiyou Department Store), Chaoyang District
  朝阳区光华西里 6 号楼北侧，贵友大厦往北 400 米
- +86 10 6593 3394, 6584 2627

Wen Ru Xin Ju Teahouse 文汝馨居
- 10 West of SOHO, Chaoyang District
  朝阳区现代城西侧 10 号
- +86 10 8580 4341

Bars and Clubs

Cafes and bars provide an alternative to traditional Chinese restaurants and teahouses. Apart from Starbucks, most cafes have tea and simple meals. Naturally, the city bars are central to Beijing's quality nightlife. Large bars have performances most nights and the main bar areas in Sanlitun (near the Workers' Stadium), Houhai, Shichahai, Workers' Stadium, Chaoyang Park, Asia Games Village (Yanyuncun) and the university area in the Haidian District are really worth checking out. New popular places include Yuandadu Bar Street, Xingbalu Bar Street.

A new bar street opened in the Yuandadu Relic Park area in northeast Beijing late in 2004. Over 20 bars and restaurants are located in a picturesque setting along a canal that runs through Yuandadu park.

Newly devised, the area is already a popular hit with young Chinese people who travel from all part of the city to party there. Using the theme of the Yuan Dynasty, Yuandadu offers a fresh alternative for students and locals alike.

Situated near Lady's Street, just opposite centrally located Kunlun Hotel and Lufthansa Centre, Xingbalu Bar Street is a recent and welcome addition to Beijing's nightlife. All these new areas in the city offer many alternatives for those hunting the trendiest spot to kick back or get down. Near by, Laitai's (Lady's Street) flower and plant stores offers the chance to go completely crazy and buy a million red roses presented later to the one you love in the bar of your choice!! Snack food and dining is also available in the area.

Beijing is a very atmospheric city at night with a great variety of trendy spots to choose from.

Angel Club 唐会酒吧
- 6 Gongti Xi Lu, Chaoyang District
  朝阳区工体西路 6 号
- +86 10 6552 8888

Babyface
- 6 Gongti Xi Lu, Chaoyang District
  朝阳区工体西路 6 号
- +86 10 6551 9081

Big Easy Bar & Restaurant
快乐站餐厅酒吧
- 1 Nongzhanguan Nanlu, South Gate of Chaoyang Park, Chaoyang District
  朝阳区农展馆南路1号朝阳公园南门东侧
- +86 10 6508 6776

Boys and Girls 男孩女孩
- Sanlitun Bar Street, Chaoyang District
  朝阳区三里屯酒吧街
- +86 10 6416 6776

Cappuccino Club 卡布基诺酒吧
Provides French and Italian-style coffee & free wireless Internet.
- North end of Sanlitun Bar Street,

Chaoyang District
朝阳区三里屯酒吧街北口
- +86 10 6417 7035

CD Café CD 咖啡屋
- South of Agriculture Exhibition Center, East Third Ring Road, Chaoyang District
  朝阳区东三环路农展馆南侧
- +86 10 6501 8877

Centro 炫酷
- 1/F, Kerry Center Hotel, 1 Guanghua Lu, Chaoyang District
  朝阳区光华路嘉里中心饭店 1 层
- +86 10 6561 8833, ext.42

Charlie 查理酒吧
- B1, Jianguo Hotel, 5, Jianguomen Wai Dajie, Chaoyang District
  朝阳区建国饭店
- +86 10 6500 2233, ext.8038

Club Banana 巴那那
- Scitech Hotel, Chaoyang District
  朝阳区赛特饭店
- +86 10 6528 3636

Club Look 乐库

📍 4 Gongti Bei Lu, Chaoyang District
朝阳区工体北路 4 号

☎ +86 10 6506 6761

Durty Nellie's Irish Pub
爱尔兰酒吧

📍 B8, Dongsanhuanbei Lu,
Chaoyang District
朝阳区东三环北路乙 8 号

☎ +86 10 6593 5050

Galleria Jazz Bar 佳利廊酒吧

📍 1/F NovotelXinqiao Beijing,
Dongcheng District
北京新侨诺富特饭店一层

☎ +86 10 6513 3366, ext. 2014,15

Get Lucky Bar 豪运酒吧

📍 Oriental Laicai world Nuren Jie,
Chaoyang District
朝阳区女人街莱太花街星路吧酒吧街内

☎ +86 10 8448 3335

Havana Café 哈瓦那

📍 Near the north gate of the Workers
Stadium, Chaoyang District
朝阳区工体北门外

☎ +86 10 6586 6166

Here Bar 这里吧

📍 97 Nan Luo Gu Xiang, Dongcheng District
东城区南锣鼓巷 97 号

☎ +86 10 8401 4246

The Tree 隐蔽的树

📍 43 Beisanlitun Nan, Chaoyang District
朝阳区北三里屯南 43 号

☎ +86 10 6415 1954

Hou Hai Cafe and Bar 后海酒吧

📍 20 South Houhai, Xicheng District
北京西城区后海南沿 20 号

☎ +86 10 6613 7825

John Bull Pub 尊伯英式酒吧

📍 44 Guanghua Lu, Chaoyang District
朝阳区光华路 44 号

☎ +86 10 6532 5905

Latinos 拉丁舞俱乐部

📍 Chaoyang Park South Gate,
Chaoyang District
朝阳区朝阳公园南门

☎ +86 10 6507 9898

Lotus Blue 兰莲花

📍 Inside Louts Lane, Ping'an street,
Xicheng District
西城区平安大街什刹海荷花市场内

☎ +86 10 6617 2599

Nameless Highland Bar 无名高地酒吧

📍 Building 14, area 1, Anhuili, Yayuncun,
Chaoyang District
朝阳区亚运村安慧里 1 区 14 号楼

☎ +86 10 6489 1613/2122

Suzie Wong 苏茜黄俱乐部

📍 West Gate of Chaoyang Park,
Chaoyang District
朝阳区朝阳公园西门

☎ +86 10 6593 6049

The Goose & Duck Pub & Restaurant
鹅和鸭西餐厅

📍 1 Greenlake Nanlu, Chaoyang Gongyuan
Xilu, Chaoyang District
朝阳区朝阳公园西路碧湖居南路 1 号

☎ +86 10 6538 1827

Passby Bar 过客酒吧

📍 108 Nanluogu Xiang, Dongcheng District
东城区南锣鼓巷 108 号

☎ +86 10 6406 2243

Tango 糖果

📍 79 Hepingli Xijie, Dongcheng District
东城区和平里西街 79 号

☎ +86 10 6428 2288

The Bridge 桥吧

📍 Northeast Yindingqiao, Xicheng District
西城区银锭桥 14 号

☎ +86 10 6615 1366

The Loft 藏酷

📍 4 Gonti Beilu, Chaoyang District
朝阳区工体北路 4 号

☎ +86 10 6501 7501

Vanilla 香草天空

📍 43 Yandai Xiejie next to Lotus and across
from Lotus Root, Xicheng District
烟袋斜街 43 号

☎ +86 10 6402 6440

8 Gua 8 卦

📍 6 C Houhai Ya'er Hutong, Xicheng District
西城区后海鸦儿胡同丙 6 号

☎ +86 10 6401 8080

Chinese Style

Beijing Local Cuisine

Beijinggong Zhengwei Restaurant
北京宫正味大酒楼
- 🏠 130 Chaoyangmennei Dajie, Dongcheng District
  东城区朝内大街 130 号
- ☎ +86 10 6523 6320

Garden View
首都食府
- 🏠 Capital Hotel (Lobby Level), 3 Qianmen Dongdajie, Dongcheng District
  东城区前门东大街 3 号首都大酒店一层
- ☎ +86 10 6512 9988, ext. 3066

Royal City
皇城食府中餐厅
Imperial and Cantonese dishes in traditional courtyards
- 🏠 Inside Changpuhe Park, Nanchizi Dajie, Dongcheng District
  东城区南池子大街菖蒲河公园内
- ☎ +86 10 8511 5142/3

Beijing Roast Duck

Quanjude Roast Duck Restaurant
北京全聚德烤鸭店
The best traditional Peking roast duck in town!
- 🏠 32 Qianmen Dajie, Chongwen District
  崇文区前门大街 32 号
- ☎ +86 10 6511 2418

Pianyi Fang Roast Duck Restaurant
便宜坊烤鸭店
- 🏠 2B Chongwenmenwai Dajie, Chongwen District
  崇文区崇外大街甲 2 号
- ☎ +86 10 6712 0505

Duck King
鸭王烤鸭店
Slightly different from the rest, insteaf of the flat pancakes you can order griddle cakes in which to put your duck.
- 🏠 24 Jianguomenwai Dajie, Chaoyang District
  朝阳区建国门外大街 24 号
- ☎ +86 10 6515 6908

Dadong Peking Duck
大董烤鸭店
Traditional Peking roast duck. Convenient

location near Sanlitun
- 🏠 Building 3, Tuanjiehu Beikou, Chaoyang District
  朝阳区团结湖北口 3 号楼
- ☎ +86 10 6582 4003

Cantonese Cuisine

Ah Yat Abalone
阿一鲍鱼
- 🏠 1 Jianguomenwai Dajie, Chaoyang District
  朝阳区建外大街 1 号
- ☎ +86 10 6508 9613
- 🏠 2/F, New Century Hotel, 6, Capital Stadium Nanlu, Haidian District
  海淀区首都体育馆南路6号新世纪饭店2层
- ☎ +86 10 6849 1315

Chao Hao Wei
潮好味
Excellent seafood dishes such as abalone, shark's fin
- 🏠 7/F, Landao West Wing, 10 Chaoyangmenwai Dajie, chaoyang District
  朝阳区朝外大街 10 号蓝岛西区 7 层
- ☎ +86 10 6599 5329

Dynasty Restaurant
满福楼
Elegantly decorated dining hall and VIP rooms. An array of specialties prepared by a renowned Hong Kong chef, which include abalone, shark's fin, Hong Kong dim sum and freshly caught seafood dishes.
- 🏠 4/F, Jingguang New World Hotel, chaoyang District
  朝阳区京广新世界饭店四层
- ☎ +86 10 6597 8888, ext. 2599

Huang Du
皇都中餐厅
Up scale Cantonese cuisine, in a traditional Chinese setting inspired by the Forbidden City.
- 🏠 Radisson SAS Hotel, 6A, East Beisanhuan Road, Chaoyang District
  朝阳区北三环东路甲 6 号皇家大饭店
- ☎ +86 10 6466 3388, ext. 3423

Noble Court
悦庭
Serves the most exquisite Cantonese cuisine - China's finest for subtlety, distinctive flavor and artistic presentation, prepared by master

chefs from Hong Kong.

📍 Grand Hyatt Beijing, 1 East Chang'an Jie, Dongcheng District
东城区东方君悦大酒店，东长安街 1 号

☎ +86 10 85181 234, ext. 3822

Royal Restaurant
盛华瑄

📍 Tianlun Dynasty Hotel, Dongcheng District
东城区王府井大街天伦王朝饭店

☎ +86 10 6513 8888, ext.8168

Capital Hotel Vigor Abalone Restaurant
首都大酒店威哥鲍翅酒楼

📍 Capital Hotel (2nd Floor), 3 Qianmen Dongdajie, Dongcheng District
东城区前门大街 3 号首都大酒店二层

☎ +86 10 6512 9988, ext. 3571

Shun Feng
顺峰餐厅

📍 16 Dongsanhuan Beilu, Chaoyang District
朝阳区东三环北路 16 号

☎ +86 10 6507 0554

Sui Yuan
随园

Enjoy the culinary delights of Cantonese cuisine including a selection of live seafood, freshly made Dim Sum and famous Beijing roast duck

📍 Hilton Hotel, 1 Dongfang Lu, Dongsanhuan Beilu, Chaoyang District
朝阳区东三环北路东方路1号希尔顿饭店

☎ +86 10 6466 2288, ext. 7416

Tai Pan Restaurant
林一品

Famous for its shark's fin soup and abalone (shellfish) cooking. Additional free dishes

📍 1/F, Sanquan Apartment, 38 Maizidian Jie, Chaoyang District
朝阳区麦子店街 38 号三全公寓首层

☎ +86 10 6507 7328

Ziyixuan Restaurant
紫怡轩鲍翅楼

📍 3/F, Building B, East Gate Plaza, Dongzhong Jie, Dongcheng District
东城区东中街 29 号东环广场 B 座三层

☎ +86 10 6418 2001

Guizhou Cuisine

Three Guizhouren
三个贵州人

📍 3 Guanghua Xi Li, Chaoyang District
朝阳区光华西里 3 号

☎ +86 10 6507 4761

Hot Pot

Huang Cheng Lao Ma
皇城老妈

📍 South of the Motorola Building, Chaoyang District
朝阳区大北窑摩托拉大厦后

☎ +86 10 6779 8801, 6779 7742

Jin Shan Cheng Chongqing Hot Pot
金山城重庆火锅

Popular Sichuan style spicy hot pot

📍 15 Xiaoyun Road, Chaoyang District
朝阳区霄云路 15 号

☎ +86 10 8451 8912

Home Cooking

Our Home
咱家的菜馆

📍 3/F, 27 Dongzhimenwai Dajie, Chaoyang District
朝阳区东直门外大街 27 号三楼

☎ +86 10 6467 2571

Xiao Wang's Home Restaurant
北京小王府

Homestyle, Chinese cooking, particularly suited to the Western palate.

📍 Building 2, Guanghua Dongli, Chaoyang District
朝阳区光华东里 2 号楼

☎ +86 10 6591 3255, 6594 3602

📍 4 A, Gongti Dong Lu, Chaoyang District
朝阳区工体东路甲 4 号赛克赛思俱乐部一层

☎ +86 10 6592 8777

Hubei/Hunan Cuisine

Liujiaguo Restaurant
刘家锅酒楼

📍 19 Nanheyan Dajie, Dongcheng District
东城区南河沿大街 19 号

☎ +86 10 6524 1487

Xiang E Qing
湘鄂情

📍 A2 Dinghuisi, Fucheng Lu, Haidian District
海淀区阜成路定慧寺甲 2 号

☎ +86 10 8813 5388

Imperial Cuisine

Bai Jia Da Zhai Men
白家大宅门
- 29, Suzhoulu, Haidian District
  海淀区苏州街 29 号
- +86 10 6265 8851

Fangshan Restaurant
仿膳饭庄
Traditional palace cuisine in the beautiful setting of Beihai Park.
- Inside the Beihai Park , 1 Wenjin Street, Xicheng District
  西城区文津街 1 号北海公园内
- +86 10 64011889

Li Jia Cai
厉家菜
- 11 Yangfang Hutong, Deshengmennei Dajie, Xicheng District
  西城区德胜门内大街羊房胡同 11 号
- +86 10 6618 0107

Pavilion of Listening to Orioles
听鹂馆
Traditional palace cuisine in the beautiful scenery of the Summer Palace
- Inside the Summer Palace, Haidian District
  海淀区颐和园内
- +86 10 6288 1955, 6288 1608

Jiangsu and Zhejiang

Gu Yue Ren Jia
古越人家
- Asian Games Village, Chaoyang District
  朝阳区亚运村名人国际大酒店以北
- +86 10 6497 0422

Minghui Teahouse
明慧茶院
- Dajue Temple, Bei'anhe, Haidian District
  海淀区北安河大觉寺
- +86 10 6246 1567

Peach Blossoms
荟芳阁
- Capital Hotel, 3 Qianmendong Dajie, Dongcheng District
  东城区前门东大街 3 号首都大酒店
- +86 10 6512 9988

Suzhe Restaurant
苏浙酒楼国贸店
- 2/F, West Wing, China World Trade Center, Chaoyang District
  国贸西楼二层
- +86 10 6605 3132

Kongyiji
孔乙己
- South bank of Houhai Shichahai, Deshengmen, Xicheng District
  西城区德胜门什刹海后海南岸
- +86 10 6618 4915

Kejia Cuisine

Lao Hanzi
老汉字
- Shichahai East Bank, Xicheng District
  西城区什刹海东岸
- +86 10 6404 2259

Minority Delicacies

A Fun Ti Hometown Restaurant
阿凡提餐厅
An exciting restaurant with Xinjiang cuisine; crazy music & dance show
- A2 Houguaibang Hutong, Chaoyangmennei Dajie
  朝阳门内大街后拐棒胡同甲 2 号
- +86 10 6525 1071

South Silk Road
茶马古道
Yunnan Cuisine
- 3/F, Tower D, SOHO, Jianguo Lu Chaoyang District
  朝阳区建国路现代城 D 座 3 楼
- +86 10 8580 4286

Grassland In The Sky
(Teng Ge Li Ta La)
腾格里塔拉
Typical Mongolian food
- 2 Wanshou Lu, Haidian District
  海淀区万寿路 2 号
- +86 10 6815 0808, 6828 8322

Makyeame Tibetan Restaurant & Bar
玛吉阿米西藏风情餐吧
- 2/F, Xiushui Nan Jie, Jianguomen Wai, Chaoyang District
  朝阳区建国门外秀水南街 11 号二层
- +86 10 6506 9616

Zhuo Ma Tibetan Restaurant
卓玛藏餐吧
- 18 Jing'anli Dongjie, Chaoyang District
  朝阳区静安庄静安里东街 18 号
- +86 10 8448 3090

Shanxi Cuisine

Noodle Loft Shanxi Cuisine
面酷山西食艺

📍 20, Xi Dawang Lu, Chaoyang District
朝阳区西大望路 20 号, 现代城往南

☎ +86 10 6774 9950

Shanghai Cuisine

Hu Jiang Xiang Man Lou
沪江香满楼食府

📍 34, Dongsi Shitiao, Dongcheng District
东城区东四十条 34 号

☎ +86 10 6403 1368

Jing Yi Zhou
静颐洲

📍 2/F, Building B, East Gate Plaza,
Dongcheng District
东城区东中街 29 号东环广场 B 座二层

☎ +86 10 6418 1072

Lao Zheng Xing
老正兴饭庄

Located in Qianmen Street, Old Shanghai
cuisine & well known Chinese brand.

📍 46 Qianmen Dajie, Chongwen District
崇文区前门大街 46 号

☎ +86 10 6702 2686

Lubolang Restaurant
绿波廊

📍 Landmark Tower, 8, Dongsanhuan Beilu,
Chaoyang District
朝阳区东三环北路 8 号亮马河大厦

☎ +86 10 6590 0510

📍 17 Dongsanhuan Nanlu, Chaoyang District
朝阳区东三环南路 17 号京瑞大厦二层

☎ +86 10 6765 4845

**Shanghai Restaurant at
Hotel Kunlun**
昆仑饭店上海餐厅

Local Shanghai chef brings unforgettable
Shanghai cuisine to Beijing

📍 2 Xinyuan Nanlu, Chaoyang District
朝阳区新源南路 2 号

☎ +86 10 6590 3388, ext.5394

Sichuan Cuisine

Fei Teng Yu Xiang
沸腾鱼乡

📍 A8 Xinyuan Nanli, Chaoyang District
朝阳区新源南里甲 8 号

☎ +86 10 8455 2333

Red Capital Club
新红资俱乐部

Sophisticated atmosphere offering the
discreet ambience and charm of a private
club; a shrine to the early days of the
People Republic.

📍 66 Dongsi Jiutiao, Dongcheng District
东城区东四九条 66 号

☎ +86 10 6402 7151, 8401 8886

Sichuan Restaurant
四川饭店

Historical restaurant offering Sichuan cuisine

📍 Inside the Palace of Prince Gong, A14
Liuyin Jie, Xicheng District
西城区柳荫街甲 14 号恭王府花园内

☎ +86 10 6615 6924, 6615 6925

South Beauty
俏江南

📍 L220, West Wing, China World Trade
Center, Chaoyang District
朝阳区国贸中心大厦西楼 2 层 L220

☎ +86 10 6505 0809, 6505 2288 ext. 80220

📍 2/F, Manhattan Center Building, 6
Chaoyangmen Beidajie, Dongcheng District
东城区朝阳门北大街 6 号万泰北海大厦
二层 (港澳中心瑞士酒店南侧)

☎ +86 10 8528 2331, 8528 2330

📍 19 24, Fl, Henderson Center,
Dongcheng District
东城区恒基中心大厦首层

☎ +86 10 6518 7603, 6518 7604

📍 B1 Level North Side, Kerry Centre,
Chaoyang District
朝阳区嘉里中心商场 B1 层北侧

☎ +86 10 8529 9458, 8529 9459

📍 3/F, Pacific Century Place, 2, Gongti
Beilu, Chaoyang District
朝阳区工体北路甲 2 号盈科中心三层

☎ +86 10 6539 3502, 6539 3503

📍 Sunshine Square, 68 Anli Lu, Asian
Games Village, Chaoyang District
朝阳区亚运村安利路 68 号阳光广场首
层东侧门

☎ +86 10 6495 1201, 6495 1202

📍 Tower A, North Side, Raycom Info Tech
Park, 2, Kexueyuan Nan Lu, Haidian District
海淀区科学院南路2号融科资讯中心A座北侧

☎ +86 10 8286 1698, 8286 1699

Xi He Ya Ju Restaurant
羲和雅居酒楼

Courtyard restaurant serving great food in

natural surroundings.

☎ Northeast Corner of Ritan Park,
Chaoyang District
朝阳区日坛公园东北角

☎ +86 10 8561 7643

Xielaosong Restaurant
蟹老宋香锅

☎ 8A, Nansanhuan Dong Lu, Fengtai District
丰台区南三环东路甲 8 号

☎ +86 10 6760 5668

Yu Xiang Restaurant
渝乡人家

☎ 4/F, Union Plaza, Chaoyangmen Wai
Dajie, Chaoyang District
朝阳区朝外大街联合大厦 5 层

☎ +86 10 6588 3841

Yuxin Restaurant
渝信酒楼

Popular Sichuan cuisine with reasonable
prices.

☎ 1/F & Basement of Jingtai Mansion, 24
Jianguomenwai Dajie, Chaoyang District
朝阳区建国门外大街24号京泰大厦一层

☎ +86 10 6515 6588

Vegetarian

Still Thoughts Vegetarian Restaurant
静思素食坊

☎ 18A Dafosi Dongjie, Dongcheng District
东城区大佛寺东街甲 18 号

☎ +86 10 6400 8941

Beijing Green Tianshi Vegetarian Restaurant
绿色天食餐厅

High quality vegetarian dishes and best-
known vegetarian restaurant in Beijing.

☎ 57 5 Dengshikou, Dongcheng District
东城区灯市口 57 5 号

☎ +86 10 6524 2349

Gong De Lin
功德林素菜饭庄

Highly favoured by Buddhists, dishes
prepared from secret recipes unique to Gong
De Lin.

☎ 158 Qianmennan Dajie, Chongwen District
崇文区前门南大街 158 号

☎ +86 10 6702 0867

Lotus In Moonlight
荷塘月色

The dishes combine the flavours of
Huaiyang, Chuan, Lu and Yue. Pure
vegetarian restaurant.

☎ Building 12, Liuyingnanli,
Chaoyang District
朝阳区柳营南里小区 12 号楼

☎ +86 10 6465 3299

Taiwan Cuisine

Bellagio
鹿港小镇

☎ 35, Xiaoyunlu, Chaoyang District
朝阳区霄云路 35 号

☎ +86 10 8451 9988

Western Style

American

Astor Grill
艾斯特扒房

☎ 3/F St. Regis Hotel Apartment, 21
Jianguomenwai Dajie, Chaoyang District
朝阳区建外大街 21 号国际俱乐部饭店
公寓三层

☎ +86 10 6460 6688, ext. 2637

Grandma's Kitchen
祖母的厨房

☎ A11 Xiushui Nanjie, Jianguomenwai,
Chaoyang District
朝阳区建外秀水街甲 11 号

☎ +86 10 5869 3055

Hard Rock Cafe
硬石餐厅

☎ Landmark Towers, East Third Ring
Road, Chaoyang District
朝阳区东三环亮马河大厦

☎ +86 10 6590 6688, ext. 2571

Louisiana
路易斯安那

Offers unique Cajun cuisine for lunch and
dinner along with an extensive selection of
imported wines.

☎ 2/F, Hilton Hotel, 1 Dongfang Lu,
Dongsanhuan Beilu, Chaoyang District
朝阳区东三环北路东方路1号希尔顿饭
店二层

☎ +86 10 6466 2288, ext. 7420

Royal Cafe
皇家咖啡厅
Offering a variety of light Mediterranean snacks and some classic Scandinavian dishes.

📍 2/F Radisson SAS Hotel, 6A, East Beishanhuan Road, Chaoyang District
朝阳区北三环东路甲6号皇家大饭店二层

☎ +86 10 6466 3388, ext. 3440

Schiller's
西乐酒屋
📍 Opposite the Kempinski Hotel, Chaoyang District
朝阳区燕沙商城北侧

☎ +86 10 6461 9276

Friday's
星期五餐厅
Beijing's Fab American theme restaurant

📍 Eagle Run Mansion,19 Dongsanhuan Beilu, Chaoyang District
朝阳区东三环北路 19 号华鹏大厦

☎ +86 10 6597 5037

The Texan Bar & Grill
德克萨斯扒房
Known as the best steak house in town, the restaurant serves prime steaks to suit the client's appetite - and at great prices! It also offers a wide variety of Tex Mex specialties including Margaritas!

📍 Holiday Inn Lido Beijing , Jichang Road, Jiang Tai Road, Chaoyang District
首都机场路蒋台路丽都假日饭店

☎ +86 10 6437 6688, ext. 1849

French

Cuisine Gallery
凯涛西餐厅
The only creperie in Beijing, providing salted and sweet gourmet pancakes, nicely complemented with tartiflette and moules marinieres on the new brasserie menu.

📍 2/F, Novotel Xinqiao, 2 Dongjiaominxiang, Dongcheng District
东城区东交民巷 2 号新侨饭店二层

☎ +86 10 6513 3366, ext. 2201

FLO
福楼
One of the finest Gallic spots in town; Authentic French food.

📍 2/F, Rainbow Plaza, Chaoyang District
朝阳区长虹桥东北角隆博广场二层

☎ +86 10 6595 5139

Gaddi's
凯帝斯法餐厅
📍 1/F, C 2, Oriental Plaza, Dongcheng District
东城区东方广场 C2 座 1 层

☎ +86 10 8518 3768

Justine
📍 1/F, Jianguo Hotel, Chaoyang District
朝阳区建国饭店一层

☎ +86 10 6500 2233, ext. 8039

La Cite French Restaurant
紫禁阁西餐厅
Authentic French cuisine, 100 yuan per head business lunch.

📍 115 Nanchizi Dajie, Dongcheng District
东城区南池子大街 115 号

☎ +86 10 8511 5142/3

La Terrasse
拉德莱斯
📍 B38 Kerry Centre, 1 Guanghualu, Chaoyang District
朝阳区嘉里中心 B38

☎ +86 10 8529 9419

Le Cabernet Wine Bar & Bistro
卡本妮红酒吧
📍 Novotel Peace Hotel, 3 Goldfish Lane, Dongcheng District
东城区金鱼胡同 3 号和平宾馆

☎ +86 10 6512 8833, ext. 6621

Le Petit Gourmand
小美食家
📍 South Building 10, Beisanlitun Lu, Chaoyang District
朝阳区北三里屯路南十楼下

☎ +86 10 6416 7154

Louisiana Restaurant
路易斯安那餐厅
📍 Hilton Hotel, 1 Dongfang Lu, Dongsanhuan Beilu, Chaoyang District
朝阳区东三环北路东方路1号希尔顿饭店

☎ +86 10 6466 2288

Maxim's
马克西姆
Classical French cuisine

📍 2 Chongwenmenxi Dajie
崇文区崇文门西大街 2 号

☎ +86 10 6512 1992

Morel Restaurant & Cafe
莫劳龙玺西餐

📍 Opposite the north gate of the Worker´s Gymnasium, Chaoyang District
朝阳区工人体育馆北门对面

☎ +86 10 6416 8802

Sit
八十坐空间

📍 4 Jiuxianqiao Lu, Dashanzi, Chaoyang District
朝阳区酒仙桥路 4 号

☎ +86 10 8456 4823

German

Blockhouse
布洛克

📍 2 Guandongdian Nanjie, Guanghualu, Chaoyang District
朝阳区光华路关东店 2 号

☎ +86 10 6561 6166

Der Landgraf
兰特伯爵

📍 A2 Pufanglu, Fangzhuang, Fengtai District
丰台区方庄蒲方路甲 2 号

☎ +86 10 6768 2664

Paulaner Brauhaus
普拉纳

📍 1/F, Kempinski Hotel, Chaoyang District
朝阳区凯宾斯基饭店一层

☎ +86 10 6465 3388, ext. 5731

Schiller's 2
大明西餐厅

📍 1 Liangmahe Nanlu, Chaoyang District
朝阳区亮马河南路 1 号

☎ +86 10 8562 6439

Italian

Adria
亚的里亚

📍 16, Xinyuan Jie, Chaoyang District
朝阳区新源街 16 号

☎ +86 10 6460 0896

📍 River Garden Villa, Shunyi District
顺义区裕京花园内

☎ +86 10 8046 5327

Assaggi
尝试

📍 1 Sanlitun Beixiaojie, Chaoyang District
朝阳区三里屯北小街 1 号

☎ +86 108454 4508

Agrilandia
意大利农场

📍 Nanguoyuan Shilipu, Shunyi District
顺义十里堡南果园

☎ +86 10 6947 3133

Danieli's
丹尼艾丽

Regional southern Italian cooking and wines great prices, great reputation!!

📍 21 Jianguomenwai Dajie, St. Regis Hotel, Chaoyang District
朝阳区国际俱乐部饭店

☎ +86 10 6460 6688, ext. 2440

Da Giorgio
意餐厅

📍 Grand Hyatt Beijing, Dongcheng District
东城区东方君悦大酒店

☎ +86 10 8518 1234, ext. 3628

Grappa's
桂葡诗

📍 2/F, Pacific Century Place, 2A, Gongti Beilu, Chaoyang District
朝阳区工体北路甲 2 号

☎ +86 10 6539 3586

Mediterraneo
地中海

📍 1 Sanlitun Beijie, Chaoyang District
朝阳区三里屯北街 1 号

☎ +86 10 6415 3691

Pinocchio Italian Restaurant
意大利餐厅

Thin and deep pan pizzas with fabulous toppings are the main draw; choice of other goodies like pastas, salads, seafood and vegetarian dishes. Variety of European dishes too, including soups and hearty main dishes.

📍 Holiday Inn Lido Beijing, Jichang Road, Jiang Tai Road, Chaoyang District
朝阳区首都机场蒋台路丽都假日饭店

☎ +86 10 6437 6688, ext. 3812

Ristorante Bologna
波罗尼亚餐厅

📍 Capital Hotel (20th Floor), 3 Qianmen Dongdajie, Dongcheng District
东城区前门东大街 3 号首都大酒店

☎ +86 10 6512 9988, ext. 3688

Coffee House

Atrium Cafe
连天阁

East meets West buffet served daily; breakfast, lunch and dinner; 24 hour a la carte dining.

📍 Hilton Hotel, 1 Dongfang Lu, Dongsanhuan Beilu, Chaoyang District
朝阳区东三环北路东方新1号希尔顿饭店

☎ +86 10 6466 2288, ext. 7406

Café ADRIA
欧意风休闲餐厅

📍 9 West Street, Lady's Street, Chaoyang District
朝阳区女人街西街9号

☎ +86 10 8454 0797

Cafe California
加州咖啡厅

With international round-the-clock fare.

📍 Rosedale Hotel & Suites, 8 Jiangtai Xilu, Chaoyang District
朝阳区蒋台西路8号

☎ +86 10 6436 2288 ext. 2617

Café Renaissance
文荟西餐厅

📍 7/F, Jingguang New World Hotel, Chaoyang District
朝阳区京广新世界饭店七层

☎ +86 10 6597 8888, ext. 2513

Chatterbox Coffee House
话匣子咖啡厅

📍 Capital Hotel (Lobby Level), 3 Qianmen Dongdajie, Dongcheng District
东城区前门东大街3号首都大酒店

☎ 6512 9988, ext. 3141

Grand Café
凯菲厅

Showcased by superb lunch and dinner buffets, presenting western and oriental flavors with genuine French, Italian and Beijing home style cooking.

📍 Grand Hyatt Beijing, 1 East Chang'an Avenue, Dongcheng District
东城区东长安街1号东方君悦大酒店

☎ +86 10 8518 1234, ext. 3628

Kosmo

📍 225 Chaoyangmennei Dajie, Chaoyang District
朝阳区朝内大街225号

☎ +86 10 8400 1567

La River Gauche Coffee Shop Bar
左岸咖啡屋 . 酒吧

📍 11 Shicha Qianhai Beiyan, Xicheng District
西城区前海北沿11号

☎ +86 10 6612 9300

Pizza

Domino
达米乐比萨

📍 Fuxinglu 23, Haidian District
海淀区复兴路23号

☎ +86 10 6821 1118

Mr Pizza
米斯特比萨

📍 23 Chengfulu Haidian District
海淀区成府路23号

☎ +86 10 8238 8807

Pizza Hut
必胜客

📍 29 Dongzhimenwai Dajie, Chaoyang District
朝阳区东直门外大街29号

☎ +86 10 6465 2976

Ice Cream

DQ/OJ Treat Centre
DQ 冰淇淋

DQ can be found in most quality shopping centers across the city. Can also be found near almost any Yoshinoiya (Jiyejia) fast food outlets.

📍 CC01, Oriental Plaza, 1 East Chang An Avenue, Dongcheng District
东城区东长安街1号东方广场CC01

Sandwich Shops

German Food Center
德国食品店

📍 15, Zaoying Beili, Maizidian, Chaoyang District
朝阳区麦子店枣营北里面15号

☎ +86 10 6591 9370

Gourmet
美食店

📍 1/F, West Office Building, China World Hotel, Chaoyang District
朝阳区中国大饭店西办公楼一层

☎ +86 10 6505 2266, ext. 43

Kempi Deli
凯宾美食廊

📍 1/F, Kempinski Hotel, Chaoyang District
朝阳区凯宾斯基饭店一层

☎ +86 10 6465 3388, ext. 5741

La Brioche
娜比奥糕饼店

📍 1/F, Novotel Peace, 3 Jinyu Hutong, Dongcheng District
东城区金鱼胡同 3 号和平宾馆一层

☎ +86 10 6512 8833, ext. 7601

Lido Deli
丽都小美食

📍 1/F, Holiday Inn Lido Beijing, Chaoyang District

朝阳区丽都假日饭店一层

☎ +86 10 6437 6688, ext. 1542

Schlotzsky's
斯乐斯基

📍 1/F, Oriental Plaza, Dongcheng District
东城区东方广场新天地一层

☎ +86 10 8518 6810

Steakhouse

Outback Steakhouse
澳拜客牛排

📍 North Gate, East Wing, Beijing Workers' Stadium, Chaoyang District
朝阳区工体北门

☎ +86 10 6506 6608

Asian Style

Indian

Chingari
鑫格里

Indian & Thai cuisine

📍 3/F, 27 Dongzhimenwai Dajie, Chaoyang District
朝阳区东直门外大街 27 号 3 层

☎ +86 10 8448 3690

Taj Pavilion
泰姬楼

Original Indian food with good surroundings and service.

📍 China World Trade Center, L128 West Wing Office, 1 Jianguomenwai Dajie, Chaoyang District
朝阳区国贸西楼 L128

☎ +86 10 6505 5866, 6505 2288

The Tandoor
坦道印度餐厅

Indian cuisine with live dance performance

📍 Great Dragon Hotel, 2 Gongti Bei Lu, Chaoyang District
朝阳区工体北路 2 号兆龙饭店

☎ +86 10 6597 2211

Japanese

Bai Wan Shi
百万石

📍 West Gate of Chaoyang Park, Chaoyang District
朝阳区朝阳公园西门

☎ +86 10 6594 0966

Genji
源氏

The delicate and sumptuous flavors of Japan served to your table, at the Teppanyaki counter or in one of two private Tatami Rooms.

📍 2/F, Hilton Hotel, 1 Dongfang Lu, Dongsanhuan Beilu, Chaoyang District
朝阳区东三环北路东方路1号希尔顿饭店二层

☎ +86 10 6466 2288, ext. 7402

Hatsune
隐泉

📍 8A, Guanghualu, Chaoyang District
朝阳区光华路 8A 和乔大厦 C 座

☎ +86 10 6581 3939

NIHONBASHI
日本桥

📍 Unit 106, 1/F, Kerry Mall, Chaoyang District
朝阳区嘉里中心商场 1 层 106 号

☎ +86 10 6501 6665

Gion Restaurant
祇园日本餐厅

📍 2/F, Capital Hotel, 3 Qianmen Dongdajie
东城区前门东大街 3 号首都大酒店

☎ +86 10 6512 9988, ext. 3333

Sakura
樱

📍 2/F, Hotel New Otani Chang Fu Gong, 16 Jianguomenwai Dajie
朝阳区建外大街 16 号长富宫饭店二层

☎ +86 10 6512 5555, ext. 1226

Yishiyuan
伊势原
📍 1/F, Fengyuan Hotel, Jianhua Nanlu, Jianguomenwai Dajie
朝阳区建外大街建华南路11号枫园宾馆1层
☎ +86 10 6567 6685

Korean

Arirang
雅里郎
📍 1/F, Scitech Tower, 22 Jianguomenwai Dajie, Chaoyang District
朝阳区建国门外大街22号赛特大厦一层
☎ +86 10 6512 3388, ext. 32708

Sorabol
萨拉伯尔
📍 Basement, Lufthansa Center, Chaoyang District
朝阳区燕厦商场地下一层
☎ +86 10 6465 3388, ext. 5720

Malaysian

Cafe Sambal
📍 43 Doufuchi Hutong, Dongcheng District
☎ +86 10 6400 4875
东城区旧鼓楼大街豆腐池胡同43号

Russian

Moscow Restaurant
莫斯科餐厅
📍 135 Xizhimenwai Dajie, Beijing Exhibition Center, Xicheng District
西城区西直门外大街135号北京展览馆内
☎ +86 10 6835 4454

The Elephant
大笨象
📍 17, Ritan Beilu, Chaoyang District
朝阳区日坛北路17号
☎ +86 10 8561 4013

Spanish

Ashandi
阿山蒂
📍 Opposite North Gate of Worker Stadium, Chaoyang District
朝阳区工体北门对面
☎ +86 10 6416 6231

Singaporean

Sing Chinatown
牛车水食府
📍 15 Xidan Minhang Dasha, Xichang anjie, Xicheng District
西城区西长安街15号西单民航大厦

Thai

Borom Piman Thai Restaurant
泰辣椒
The first Thai restaurant in the city, serves some of the best Thai cuisine around. With a new menu and two new Chefs flown in from Bangkok, offers fine Thai cooking in a traditional Thai setting.
📍 Holiday Inn Lido Beijing , Jichang Road, Jiang Tai Road Beijing
朝阳区首都机场路蒋台路丽都假日饭店
☎ +86 10 6437 6688, ext. 2899

Pink Loft Food and Drink
粉酷东南亚新菜
📍 6 Sanlitun Nanlu, Chaoyang District
朝阳区三里屯南路6号
☎ +86 10 6506 8811

Phink Thai
京港泰式美食
📍 6 Guandongdianjie, Chaoyang Distrct
朝阳区关东店街三巷6号
☎ +86 10 6586 9726

Very Siam
非常泰
Typical Thai style and located in the peaceful ambience of an old hutong.
📍 Northwest of Yuyang Hotel, Chaoyang Distrct
朝阳区渔阳饭店西北角胡同内
☎ +86 10 8451 0031

Vietnamese

Ma Cherie
芭蕉别墅
📍 Kunlun Hotel, 2, Xinyuan Nanlu, Chaoyang District
朝阳区新源南路2号昆仑饭店
☎ +86 10 6590 5247

Nuage
庆云楼
📍 22, Qianhai Lake East Bank , Shichahai, Xicheng District
西城区什刹海前海东沿22号
☎ +86 10 6401 9581

Part F

Shopping

Wangfujing 王府井

Beijing's premier pedestrian street complete with English language bookshops, shopping malls and fashion stores galore. Here you can also find many art galleries, street performers, and delicious food stalls. Take the subway to Wangfujing.

Xidan Street 西单

Xidan Commercial Area, north of West Chang'an Avenue, offers a wide range of shopping options. Xidan has four big shopping centres (the Chung-Yo Shopping Centre, Xidan Shopping Centre, Xidan SCITECH Plaza and Capital Times Plaza) and Beijing's biggest book store, the Beijing Book Mansion.

Friendship Store 友谊商店

Located on Jianguomenwai Dajie (just east of the East Second Ring Road), the Friendship Store provides upscale traditional Chinese goods including silk clothing, jewellery, authentic furniture, quality carpets and handmade rugs. A 10-minute walk from Jianguomen Subway exit B.

📍 17 Jianwai Dajie, Chaoyang District
朝阳区建外大街 17 号
☎ +86 10 6500 3311
🕐 9 a.m.-8:30 p.m. (in winter), 9 a.m.-9 p.m. (in summer)

Hongqiao Market 红桥市场

Also known as the Pearl Market, the store offers the enthusiastic shopper more than they could wish for. Fill your basket with pearls, bespoke jewellery, jade, arts and crafts, antiques and clothing. A fish market in the basement provides the food alternatives you might need for entertaining at the weekend.

📍 16 Hongqiao Lu, opposite the East Gate of the Temple of Heaven, Chongwen District
崇文区红桥路 16 号 （天坛东门对面）
🕐 9 a.m.-6 p.m.

New Silk Market 新秀水

On any tourist list of places to visit, the old Silk Alley was a treat for bargain-hunting tourists. Today, development in the area has made way for bigger and brighter things and one of those is the New Silk Market, a composite of the traders and wares of the old alley now spread out on three floors of this comfortable, safe new building on Jianguomenwai Dajie, Beijing's main street.

As before, the New Silk Market offers great value on fine cashmere and silk of all types and designer labels are available at knock down prices. The new Silk Market keeps respectable hours, so beat the rush and get there early. Near-by shopping malls offer plenty of places to rest from your busy day's activities where you can sip designer coffee or catch a quick bite at any one of the Chinese or Western restaurants in the area.

📍 at the connection of Xiushui Dongjie and Jianwai Dajie, Chaoyang District
朝阳区秀水东街和建外大街交界处

Yashow Market 雅秀市场

Also of interest to bargain hunters in Beijing, the Yashow Market is a big draw for the tourist with some money to spend and some serious shopping to do. Centrally located, Yashow is surrounded by the bars, restaurants and cafes of the Sanlitun area, the most popular eating and drinking area for tourists in the city, which makes extended bouts of shopping even easier.

The Market itself offers every imaginable article of clothing. If it's on the market, Yashow will have it or a version of it at the very least. Try shoes on the ground floor and custom-fitted suits on the third and fashion clothes for young and old on the floors in between. Also on the lower ground floor, luggage and hats provide variety to the shopping experience.

📍 58 Gongti Beilu, Chaoyang District
朝阳区工体北路 58 号
🕐 8:30 a.m.-9 p.m.

Panjiayuan Market 潘家园市场

Known locally as the Dirt Market (or Sunday Market,) this is the place for antiques, arts and crafts and old-style furniture. A fascinating once-in-a-lifetime shopping opportunity, don't forget to haggle! Authentic, dusty, filled with curios, humorous local characters, bustle and noise! Keep a close watch on personal belongings; it can get pretty crowded.

📍 west of Panjiayuan Qiao, Chaoyang District
朝阳区潘家园桥西
🕐 Sat. and Sun., dawn to 4 p.m.

Liulichang 琉璃厂

Beijing's most well-known antique street. Find old Chinese books, traditional paintings and brushes amongst some real gems. The best place to get your very own Chinese chop or name stamp. Take the subway to Hepingmen, walk half way down Nanxinhua Jie.

📍 Hepingmenwai, Xuanwu District
宣武区和平门外

Tongli 同里

Opened in 2003, the Tongli Studio is not just a restaurant, but a bar, a shop and a gallery combined. High-quality and delicate artistic merchandise are its major attractions.

📍 Sanlitun Bar Street, Chaoyang District
朝阳区三里屯酒吧北街
☎ +86 10 6417 6668

Gaobeidian 高碑店古典家具市场

Beijing's largest antique and imitation Chinese furniture market opened since September 2004. Old furniture collected from Shanxi, Inner Mongolia and Hebei can be found here.

🌐 Gaobeidian Village, Chaoyang District
朝阳区高碑店乡

Beijing Curio City 北京古玩城

Asia's biggest curio arts and crafts trade centre, the Beijing Curio City is a four-story complex that houses scores of kitsch and curio shops and a few furniture vendors. The market specializes in antique pottery, paintings from China and foreign countries, jadeware, bone carvings, antique furniture, antique carpets, antique timepieces, pearls and jade. Many of the dealers are themselves connoisseurs and curio collectors.

🌐 21 Dongsanhua Nanlu, Chaoyang District
朝阳区东三环南路 27 号

Golden Resources Shopping Centre
金源时代购物中心

It was the first shopping mall that came close to a western standard on the Chinese mainland. The giant centre is located between Beijing's West Third and Fourth Ring roads. It has an area of 180,000 sq.m involving an investment of 3.8 billion yuan (US$47 million).

☎ + 86 10 8887 3800
🕐 10 a.m.-9 p.m.

Dongdan-Dongsi 东单 – 东四

Fascinating and exquisite small shops that line Dongdan Dajie (parallels Wangfujing Avenue on the east) cater to women and young girls!

Shopping Centres, Supermarkets and Convenience Stores

China World Shopping Mall
国贸商城
🌐 1 Jianguomenwai Dajie,
  Chaoyang District
  朝阳区建外大街 1 号
☎ +86 10 6505 2288
🕐 9 a.m.-9:30 p.m.

Lufthansa Shopping Center
燕莎友谊商城
🌐 52 Liangmaqiao Lu,
  Chaoyang District
  朝阳区亮马桥路 52 号
☎ +86 10 6465 1188
🕐 9 a.m.-10 p.m.

The Malls at Oriental Plaza
东方新天地
🌐 1 Dongchang'an Jie, Dongcheng District
  东城区东长安街 1 号
☎ +86 10 8518 6969
🕐 9 a.m.-10 p.m.

SCITECH Plaza
赛特购物中心
🌐 22 Jaingguomenwai Dajie,
  Chaoyang District
  朝阳区建外大街 22 号
☎ +86 10 6512 4488
🕐 9:30 a.m.-9 p.m.

Beijing One World Department Store
世都百货

- 99 Wangfujing Dajie,
  Dongcheng District
  东城区王府井大街 99 号
- ☎ +86 10 6526 7890
- ◉ 10 a.m.-10 p.m.

Fulllink Plaza
丰联广场

- 18 Chaowai Dajie, Chaoyang District
  朝阳区朝外大街 18 号
- ☎ +86 10 6588 1997
- ◉ 10:30 a.m.-9:30 p.m.

Beijing New World Shopping Centre
北京新世界商场

- 3 Chongwai Dajie, Chongwen District
  崇文区崇外大街 3 号
- ☎ +86 10 6508 0055
- ◉ 9 a.m.-10 p.m. (before July 10), 9:30
  a.m.-9:30 p.m. (after July 10)

Sogo
崇光百货

- 8 Xuanwumenwai Dajie,
  Xuanwu District
  宣武区宣武门外大街 8 号
- ☎ +86 10 6310 3388
- ◉ 9:30 a.m.-10 p.m.

Supermarkets and Convenience Stores

Beijing's market development has attracted the world's retail giants. You will find international brands while roaming the streets. Look out for Wal-mart, Pricemaster, Carrefour and Metro. The American-style convenience store 7-11 opened its first Beijing outlet in Dongzhimen in 2004 and has been expanding ever since. And don't forget Quick! The 100th Quick chain opened in Beijing in 2005 and the chain is expanding rapidly. Local brands like Kelong and Shanghai's Lianhua also have a share of the market. Convenience stores are now available on almost every street corner in Beijing, so you need not pack 10 suitcases when travelling to Beijing.

Culture & Arts

Peking Opera

All kinds of performances are staged in Beijing throughout the year. Peking Opera, musicals and acrobatics, ballet and other kinds of opera afford Beijingers many occasions for entertainment.

Peking Opera is a pure form of Chinese opera, dating to 1790 when four local opera troupes from Anhui Province came to Beijing to perform at the Imperial court. The tour was successful and the artists stayed. They brought with them the essence of local Hubei opera and drew on the best of *Kun Qu*, *Qin Qiang*, *Bangzi* and other local operatic forms. Over 200 years of development, Peking Opera became more assimilated and developed into a pure form of Beijing or Peking Opera. Musical instruments from other nationalities, like the *erhu* and *jing hu* were incorporated. It is called 'opera' because it includes singing, dancing, martial arts, musical arts and literature, similar to Western opera.

The four main roles in Peking Opera are *sheng*, *dan*, *jing*, *chou*. They are denoted by different markings in face make-up. Apart from *sheng* and *dan*, the different colours of the face are used for other roles, representing various characters and personalities. Therefore, the ability to read the face markings is a key to understanding the stories.

Painting and Calligraphy

Chinese calligraphy (or brush calligraphy) is an art unique to Asian cultures. Regarded as the most abstract and sublime form of art in Chinese culture, calligraphy is often thought to be most revealing of one's personality. Unlike other visual art techniques, all calligraphy is permanent and irredeemable, demanding careful planning and confident execution. While one has to conform to the defined structure of the words, the expression is often extremely creative. To exercise the imagination, but follow the laws and regulations of the craft, is its principle virtue.

The origin of Chinese painting can be traced to the patterns carved, or drawn, on bronze and pottery in prehistory. From the Han Dynasty (206 BC–AD 220), when paper was invented, Chinese painting began to develop into its present form.

Early paintings record religious iconography, such as the Buddha. During the Tang Dynasty (618–907 BC), the trend turned towards landscapes. The following dynasties revealed different characteristics: flower-and-bird paintings in the Song (AD 960–1279); ink painting and figure paintings in the Yuan (AD 1271–1368); court paintings in the Ming (AD 1368–1644) and a revival of landscape painting and the introduction of Western-style painting in the Qing (1644–1911).

Kunqu Opera

Kunqu is China's oldest, most influential folk opera, respected as the sister of the Peking Opera. On May 18, 2001, *Kunqu* was honoured by UNESCO as one of 19 outstanding forms of cultural expression in the world.

Tradition says that *Kunqu* was created by artists in the Kunshan area more than 700 years ago. Being popular in Jiangsu, *kunqu* then spread to Zhejiang and other southern provinces after the Ming Dynasty, and was improved by artists including Wei Liangfu and Liang Zhenyu. Later *kunqu* was introduced to Beijing, and became one of two official forms of drama of the imperial court before it became popular nationwide.

Kunqu's uniqueness lies in the combination of poetry, music, song and dance, making it difficult to perform but enjoyable to watch. Accompanying instruments include drums, the *san xian* and *pi pa* stringed instruments, and wind instruments such as flutes, *Shengs*, *Xiaos*. Many famous Peking Opera players were also great performers of *kunqu*. But to be a *kunqu* performer, a grasp of more skills in both song and performance were required to give a good performance in *kunqu*.

Acrobatics

The history of acrobatics in China can be traced back to the Neolithic period (more than 5,000 years ago). It is believed that acrobatics grew from self-defense skills the people practiced and later rehearsed during their leisure time, but this is not certain.

Over time, acrobatics was developed into a performance art and became known worldwide through performances along the Silk Road.

Whether old or young, educated or illiterate, to appreciation the form simply requires you to watch. There are no linguistic or cultural barriers to cross.

One thinks of the Chinese saying, "one minute on a stage costs a performer ten years of training," when watching the skill and determination of Chinese acrobats.

Porcelain

In China, pottery has long and compex history. The earliest earthenware dates to the Neolithic period, 5000 years ago, while porcelain was first made in the Han Dynasty (BC 202–AD 220).

In the world history of porcelain, Chinese Song Dynasty (AD 960–1279) porcelain is considered some of the best, because of its elegant shapes, glazes and decorations. Artists of other ages have been influenced by Song Dynasty porcelain when it comes to pot construction, the use of innovative firings and glaze making.

Lacquerware

Lacquer is a natural substance obtained from the sap of the lacquer tree, which grows in China. Before the invention of Chinese ink, lacquer was used to write.

Lacquerware has a long history that extends back to the Neolithic period. It is a hard and tar-like substance that is moisture proof and resistant to heat, acids and alkali. Its colour and lustre is highly durable lending beauty to its practical use. Beijing is one of the leading cities in the production of Chinese lacquerware.

The making of Beijing lacquerware starts with a brass or wooden body. After preparation and polishing, it is coated with between several dozen and several hundred layers of lacquer, reaching a total thickness of 5-18 millimetres. Engravers then cut into the hardened lacquer, creating "carved paintings" of landscapes, figures, and flowers and birds. It is finished by drying and polishing. Traditionaly objects to be lacqured include chairs, screens, tea tables and vases. Emperor Qianlong of the Qing Dynasty (1644–1911), an enthusiast of lacquerware, had his own coffin inlaid with lacquer.

Architecture

Chinese architecture enjoys a long history and some notable achievements and it is associated with such feats of engineering as The Great Wall. In the process of its development, superior architectural techniques and artistic design were combined to make Chinese architecture one of the three great architectural systems.

The basic features of Chinese architecture include rectangular-shaped units of space joined as a whole. Dominated by the principles of balance and symmetry, Chinese buildings tend to adhere to this rule: a main structure is its axis, with the secondary structures, positioned as two wings on either side, forming the main room and yard. Another characteristic is the wooden structural frame with pillars, beams, and earthen walls surrounding the building on three sides.

Traditional Chinese Medicine

Traditional Chinese Medicine (TCM) is a complete system of healing that emerged in China about 3,000 years ago; it has changed very little over the centuries. It's based on the holistic idea that what governs the laws of nature governs the laws of the body. By understanding one , one can understand the other. Your health, like the universe, proponents say, is subject to a constant flux between binary opposits. For example hot and cold, male and female, joy and sadness, which manifest themselves as too much or too little activity in particular organs. An imbalance between any of these forces causes a blockage in the flow of *qi* or vital energy traveling through the body, along invisible pathways known as meridians. TCM practitioners typically use acupuncture and herbs to help unblock your *qi* and bring your body back into harmony and health.

完整的文件解决方案
Total Document Solutions

- ● 专业文件服务中心
  Professional Document
  Processing Centre
- ● 打印 Printing
- ● 复印 Photocopying
- ● 装订 Binding
- ● 颜色 Colourful
- ● 传真 Fax

What's On

Theatres

Poly Plaza International Theatre 保利国际剧院
- 📍 1/F Poly Plaza, 14 Dongzhimen Nandajie, Dongcheng District
  东城区东直门南大街 14 号保利大厦 1 层
- ☎ +86 10 6500 1188, ext. 5126, 5682

Century Theatre 世纪剧院
- 📍 40 Liangmaqiao Lu, Chaoyang District
  朝阳区亮马桥路 40 号
- ☎ +86 10 6468 3311, ext. 3161

Tianqiao Theatre 天桥剧场
- 📍 30 Beiwei Road, Xuanwu District
  宣武区北纬路 30 号
- ☎ +86 10 8315 6337

Capital Theatre 首都剧场
- 📍 22 Wangfujing Dajie, Dongcheng District
  东城区王府井大街 22 号
- ☎ +86 10 6524 9847

Beijing Exhibition Theatre 北展剧场
- 📍 135 Xizhimenwai Dajie, Xicheng District
  西城区西直门外大街 135 号
- ☎ +86 10 6835 4455

Beijing North Theatre 北京北兵马司剧场
- 📍 Beibingmasi Hutong, Jiaodaokou South Street 67, Dongcheng District
  东城区交道口南街 67 号北兵马司胡同
- ☎ +86 10 6404 8021, 6406 0175

China Children's Art Theatre 中国儿童剧院
- 📍 64 Dong'anmen Dajie, west of Wangfujing, Dongcheng District
  东城区东安门大街 64 号
- ☎ +86 10 6521 1425

Concerts

The Forbidden City Concert Hall 中山音乐堂
- 📍 Zhongshan Park, immediately west of the Forbidden City, Dongcheng District
  东城区中山公园内
- ☎ +86 10 6559 8285

National Library Concert Hall 国图音乐厅
- 📍 33 South Street, Zhongguancun, Haidian District
  海淀区中关村南大街 33 号
- ☎ +86 10 8854 5348, 8854 5501

Beijing Concert Hall 北京音乐厅
- 📍 1 Beixinhua Jie, Xicheng District
  西城区北新华街 1 号
- ☎ +86 10 66055846

Peking Opera and *Kunqu* Opera

Li Yuan Theatre 梨园剧场
- 📍 Qianmen Hotel, 175 Yong'an Lu, Xuanwu District
  宣武区永安路 175 号前门饭店内
- 🕐 7:30-8:40 p.m.
- ☎ +86 10 6301 6688, ext. 8860
- 💰 40-280 yuan

Chang'an Grand Theatre 长安大戏院
- 📍 7 Jianguomennei Dajie, Dongcheng District
  东城区建国门内大街 7 号
- 🕐 7:30-9:30 p.m.
- ☎ +86 10 6510 1155
- 💰 80-300 yuan

Beijing Huguang Guildhall 湖广会馆古戏楼
- 📍 3 Hufangqiao, Xuanwu District
  宣武区虎坊桥 3 号
- 🕐 7:30-8:40 p.m.
- ☎ +86 10 6351 8284

Acrobatics and Kung fu

Chaoyang Theatre 朝阳剧场
- 📍 36 East Third Ring Road, Chaoyang District
  朝阳区东三环 36 号
- 🕐 5:15-7:15 p.m.
- ☎ +86 10 6507 2421

Universal Theatre 天地剧场
- 📍 Dongsishitiao Lijiaoqiao, Chaoyang District
  朝阳区东四十条立交桥
- 🕐 7:15 - 8:40 p.m.
- ☎ +86 10 6502 3984

The Red Theatre 红剧场
- 📍 44 Xingfu Dajie, Chongwen District
  崇文区幸福大街 44 号
- 🕐 7:30-8:50 p.m.
- ☎ +86 10 6714 2473

Dinner show

Beijing Night Show 北京之夜
Beijing Night Show was the first of its kind to offer visitors to Beijing a rare opportunity to enjoy classical Chinese art performances and traditional Chinese cuisine. The show features a wide range of Chinese artistic performance, from traditional art and music to

dancing, opera, acrobatics and traditional costume shows. There are also performances that illustrate the customs of China many ethnic minorities

- 1 Dayabao Hutong, Dongcheng District 东城区大雅宝胡同 1 号
- Mon.-Sat., 6:30 p.m.
- +86 10 6527 2814
- 180, 240, 320, 400 yuan

Art Galleries

National Art Museum of China 中国美术馆
- 1 Wusi Dajie, Dongcheng District 东城区五四大街 1 号
- 9 a.m.-5 p.m.
- +86 10 6401 7076

The Art Gallery of China Millennium Monument 中华世纪坛艺术馆
- 9 A, Fuxing Lu, Haidian District 海淀区复兴路甲 9 号
- +86 10 6851 3322

Creation Gallery 可创艺苑
- North Corner of Ritan Donglu, Chaoyang District 朝阳区日坛东路北角
- 10 a.m.-5 p.m.
- +86 10 8561 7570
- www.creationgallery.com.cn

Wan Fung Art Gallery 云峰画苑
- 136 Nanchizi Dajie, Dongcheng District 东城区南池子大街 136 号
- 9 a.m.-5 p.m.
- +86 10 6523 3320
- www.wanfung.com.cn

Fafa Gallery 发发画廊
- 2 Xiangjiang Beilu, Chaoyang District (Opposite to Riviera Garden) 朝阳区香江北路 2 号
- +86 10 8430 2587
- www.fafagallery.com

Red Gate Gallery 红门画廊
- Dongbianmen Watchtower, Chongwenmen, Chongwen District 崇文区东便门角楼
- 10 a.m.-5 p.m.
- +86 10 6525 1005
- redgategallery.com

Qin Gallery 秦昊画廊
- Huaweili 1-1-E (North of Beijing Curio City), Chaoyang District 朝阳区华威里 1-1-E
- 9:30 a.m.-7 p.m.
- +86 10 8779 0461, 58

Artists Village Gallery 画家村画廊
- North of Renzhuang Village, Songzhuang, Tongzhou District 通州区宋庄任庄村北
- 9 a.m.-12 p.m.
- +86 10 6959 5367
- artistvillagegallery.com.

Beijing Art Now Gallery 北京现在画廊
- Inside Workers' Stadium (opposite Gate 12), Chaoyang District
- Tues.-Sun., noon-8 p.m.
- +86 10 6551 1632
- +86 10 6551 1633
- angallery@vip.sina.com www.artnow.com

Imagine Gallery 想象画廊
- 300 metres east of the Tong Da Restaurant, Feijiacun Donglu off Laiguanying Donglu, Chaoyang District 朝阳区来广营东路
- +86 13910917965, +86 10 6438 5747
- Laetitia.gauden@imagine-gallery.com www.imagine-gallery.com

Conference and Exhibition Centres

China International Exhibition Centre 中国国际展览中心
- 6 Third Ring Road North, Chaoyang District 朝阳区东三环北路 6 号
- +86 10 8460 0000

Beijing Exhibition Hall 北京展览馆
- 135 Xizhimenwai Dajie, Xicheng District 西城区西直门外大街

135 号
- +86 10 6831 6677

National Agricultural Exhibition Centre 中国农业展览馆
- 16 Third Ring Road North, Chaoyang District 朝阳区东三环北路 16 号
- +86 10 6501 8877, 6509 6688

China World Exhibition Hall 国贸中心展览大厅
- 1 Jianwai Dajie, Chaoyang District 朝阳区建外大街 1 号
- +86 10 6505 228, ext. 10448

Film

Star City Cinema 新世纪影城
- Oriental Plaza, 1 Dongchang'an Jie, Dongcheng District 东城区东长安街 1 号东方广场地下一层
- +86 10 8518 6778

Sun Dong An Cinema 新东安影城
- 5th floor of Sun Dong An Plaza, 138 Wangfujing Dajie, Dongcheng District 东城区王府井大街 138 号新东安 5 层
- +86 10 6528 1838, 98

Dahua Cinema 大华电影院
- 82 Dongdan Beidajie, Dongcheng District 东城区东单北大街 82 号
- +86 10 6527 4420

UME International Cineplex 华星影城
- 44 Kexueyuan Nanlu, opposite Shuang'an Market, Haidian District 海淀区双榆树科学院南路 44 号(双安商场对面)
- +86 10 8211 5566; 8211 2851

Cherry Lane Movies
Showing Chinese films produced in the 1980s.
- An Jia Lou inside the Kent Center, 29 Liangmaqiao Lu (east of Kempinski

Hotel), Chaoyang
District
朝阳区高澜大厦红绿
灯向北 70 米路东，安
家楼肯特中心院内
☎ +86 10 139 0113 4745

Foreign Cultural Institutes

Cultural Affairs Office of
the Italian Embassy 意大利
使馆文化处
📖 2 Sanlitun Dong'er

Jie, Chaoyang District
朝阳区三里屯东二街2号
☎ +86 10 6532 2178

Cultural Affairs Office of
the Mexican Embassy
墨西哥使馆文化处
📖 5 Sanlitun Dongwu
Jie, Chaoyang District
朝阳区三里屯东五街5号
☎ +86 10 6532 2244

Cultural Affairs Office of
the Brazilian Embassy
巴西使馆文化处
📖 27 Guanghua Lu,

Chaoyang District
朝阳区光华路 27 号
☎ +86 10 6532 5282

Cultural Affairs Office of
the Canadian Embassy
加拿大使馆文化处
📖 19 Dongzhimenwai
Dajie, Chaoyang
District
朝阳区东直门外大街
19 号
☎ +86 10 6532 3536

Part I

Mother Tongue
Chinese language suggestions for visitors to the city

A word about the language...
Making an effort is more important than getting it right. This the Chinese people really appreciate. So go on, give it a go... helpful words and phrases below

Words that count

Hello >	Where is the post office? >
Nǐ hǎo	Yóujú zài nǎlǐ?
Goodbye >	**I want to buy a phone card >**
Zàijiàn	Wǒ xiǎng mǎi diàhuàkǎ
Please >	**I want to make a call to.... >**
Qǐng	Wǒ xiǎng dǎ diànhuà dào...
Thank you >	**Is there an Internet cafe? >**
Xièxiè	Běndì yǒu wǎngbā mā?
Thank you very much >	**How much is it? >**
Tài xièxièlē	Duōshǎo qián?
Yes >	**Do you have...? >**
Shìdē	Nǐ yǒu...?
No >	**I am a vegetarian >**
Méiyǒu	Wǒ chī sù
Do you understand? >	**Not too spicy >**
Dǒng mā?	Bú yào tài Là
I understand >	**Menu >**
Wǒ tīngdědǒng	Càidān
I don't understand >	**Bill >**
Wǒ tīngbùdǒng	Mǎidān
Place to eat >	**Let's eat >**
Chīfàn dē dìfāng	Chīfàn
What? >	**Beer >**
Shénmè	Píjiǔ
When? >	**Water >**
Shénmè shíhòu	Kāishuǐ
Where? >	**Coffee >**
Nǎ'r	Kāfēi
I'd like to change money >	**Tea >**
Wǒ xiǎng huànqián	Chá

Numbers

1 >	yī/yāo		**6** >	liù
2 >	èr/liǎng		**7** >	qī
3 >	sān		**8** >	bā
4 >	sì		**9** >	jiǔ
5 >	wǔ		**10** >	shí

Days of the Week

Monday >	xīngqīyī
Tuesday >	xīngqīèr
Wednesday >	xīngqīsān
Thursday >	xīngqīsì
Friday >	xīngqīwǔ
Saturday >	xīngqīliù
Sunday >	xīngqītiān

Today >
jīntiān

Tonight >
jīntiān wǎnshàng

Tommorrow >
míngtiān

My name is ... >
Wǒ dē míngzì shì ....

What's your name? >
Nǐ jiào shénmè míngzì?

I am from ... >
Wǒ cóng nǎ lái?

Where are you from? >
Nǐ shì cóng nǎ lái dē?

Part J

2008 Olympics

The Beijing 2008 Olympic Games will be a momentous event for the Chinese people, but especially for residents of Beijing, Qingdao, Qinghuangdao, Shenyang, Shanghai, and Hong Kong, venue cities for Games competitions.

By 2008, Beijing, the host city for the XXIX Olympiad, is expected to complete a major social and cultural transformation, making it one of world's most popular tourist destinations.

After Mayor Wang Qishan accepted the Olympic flag from the president of the Athens Olympic Organizing Committee in August 2004, the eyes of an expectant world turned to Beijing. The end of the Athens Olympics ushered in a new phase of Beijing's preparations for the 2008 Games.

Beijing, under the leadership of the Beijing Organizing Committee for the Games of the XXIX Olympiad (BOCOG), will stage a "high-level" Olympic Games "with distinguishing features" in 2008, which means it will be a "showcase event" for China's modern features. One of those "high-levels" involves mass participation; a great many volunteers are expected in support of the Games.

On January 14, 2005, at the Second Plenary Session of BOCOG, BOCOG President Liu Qi outlined eight criteria for a "high-level" Olympic Games: first-class infrastructure and venues, high-profile cultural events, minimal traffic congestion, professional media services and outstanding performances by local athletes.

On June 26, 2005, the 2008 Olympic slogan "One World, One Dream" was launched. It conveys the noble ideal of the people of Beijing and China to share their civilization and to create a bright future in cooperation with the world's people.

In preparation for the 2008 Games, the city has adopted the themes: "Green Olympics," "High-tech Olympics" and "People's Olympics" through which investments in the city and the Games are taking place.

Green Olympics

Making the Olympics green means apply sustainable, high-tech environmental-protection principles that involve planting, maintaining and protecting plant life and the use of state-of-the-art architectural principles, building techniques and materials in Olympic vene construction. Planting projects are expected to increase the public's awareness of the importance of natural vegetation and the need to protect the natural landscape. The "Green Olympics" is an attempt to promote this awareness and to encourage the nationwide adoption of the principles of environmental protection and resource management through the many activities of the 2008 Olympic Games.

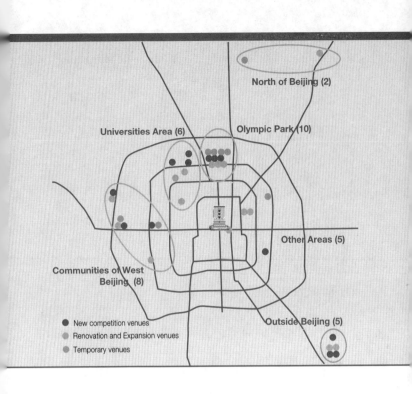

North of Beijing (2)

Universities Area (6)

Olympic Park (10)

Other Areas (5)

Communities of West Beijing (8)

Outside Beijing (5)

- ● New competition venues
- ● Renovation and Expansion venues
- ● Temporary venues

2008 Olympic Games Competition Venues (up to June, 2005)

11 New Competition Venues

No.	Venue	Sports and events	Location
1	National Stadium	Opening & Closing Ceremonies, Athletics, Football Finals (TBD)	Olympic Green
2	National Aquatics Centre	Swimming, Diving, Water Polo, Synchronized Swimming	Olympic Green
3	Beijing Shooting Range Hall	Shooting	Xiangshan Nanlu
4	Laoshan Velodrome	Cycling (Track)	Laoshan, Shijingshan District
5	Wukesong Indoor Stadium	Basketball	Wukesong Culture and Sports centre
6	National Indoor Stadium	Artistic Gymnastics, Trampoline, Handball	Olympic Green
7	Shunyi Olympic Rowing-Canoeing Park	Rowing, Canoe/Kayak (Flatwater Racing, Slalom Racing)	Mapo Village, Shunyi District
8	China Agriculture University Gymnasium	Wrestling	China Agriculture University
9	Peking University Gymnasium	Table Tennis	Peking University
10	Beijing Science & Technology University Gymnasium	Judo, Taekwondo	Beijing Science &Technology University
11	Beijing University of Technology Gymnasium	Badminton, Rhythmic Gymnastics	Beijing University of Technology

11 Exsiting Competition Venues

No.	Venue	Sports	Location
1	Fengtai Softball Field	Softball	Fengtai Sports centre
2	Workers' Indoor Arena	Boxing	Gongti road
3	Workers' Stadium	Football	Gongti road, Chaoyang District
4	Beihang University Gymnasium	Weightlifting	Beihang University
5	Olympic Sports Centre Stadium	Football, Modern Pentathlon (Running, Riding)	Olympic Sports Centre
6	Ying Tung Natatorium	Water polo, Modern Pentathlon (Swimming)	Olympic Sports Centre
7	Laoshan Mountain Bike Course	Cycling (Mountain Bike)	Laoshan, Shijingshan District
8	Beijing Shooting Range (Clay Target Field)	Shooting	Xiang shan nan lu
9	Olympic Sports Centre Gymnasium	Handball	Olympic Sports Centre
10	Capital Indoor Stadium	Volleyball	Baishiqiao, Haidian District
11	Beijing Institute of Technology Gymnasium	Volleyball	Beijing Institute of Technology

9 Temporary Competition Venues

No.	Venue	Sports	Location
1	Fencing Gymnasium (Conference Centre)	Fencing, Modern Pentathlon (Shooting & Fencing)	Olympic Green
2	Wukesong Baseball Field	Baseball	Wukesong Culture and Sports Centre
3	Olympic Green Hockey Field	Hockey	Olympic Green
4	Beach Volleyball Ground	Beach Volleyball	Chaoyang Park
5	Olympic Green Archery Field	Archery	Olympic Green
6	BMX Field	Cycling (BMX)	Laoshan, Shijingshan District
7	Triathlon Venue	Triathlon	Ming Tomb Reservoir
8	Urban Road Cycling Course	Cycling (Road Race)	TBD
9	Olympic Green Tennis Center	Tennis	Olympic Green

Interesting facts for 2008 Olympics

- The 2008 Olympic Games will begin at 8:08 p.m. on August 8, 2008, and will end on August 24.
- It is estimated that the 2008 Olympics will attract about 3 million foreign visitors, and about 30,000 journalists from around the globe will come to write and photograph the community and the Games in Beijing.
- It is anticipated that the 2008 Olympic Torch Relay will pass Mount Qomolangma.
- There will be 28 main competition sports in the 2008 Games, 26 will be held in Beijing. Sailing and equestrian events will be held in Qindao (a seaside city in Shandong Province) and Hong Kong. The other four co-host cities, all venues for football games, are in Shenyang (in Liaoning Province in Northeast China), Qinhuangdao (a seaside city in Hebei Province), Tianjin (in North China) and Shanghai (in East China.)
- About 100,000 volunteers from around the world will serve during the 2008 Olympics.

- The 2008 Olympics emblem is "Dancing Beijing"; its slogan is "One World, One Dream." It fully reflects the essence and universal values of the Olym pic spirit – Unity, Friendship, Progress, Harmony, Participa tion and Dream.
- Lenovo, a leading IT producer in China, is the first Chinese enterprise to be come one of Worldwide Olympic partners. The other eight official partners are the Bank of China, China Netcom, SINOPEC, CNPC, China Mo- bile, Volkswagen Group (China), Johnson & Johnson, Adidas and Air China. (Source: Beijing Organizing Committee for the Games of the XXIX Olympiad)

High-tech Olympics

Incorporating 387 Olympic projects, the High-tech Olympics is a citywide and a Beijing Olympics-wide plan designed to promote the development and employment of leading technologies for use in the Beijing 2008 Olympic Games.

The thirty-one competition venues in Beijing that will be used as venues for 26 of the Olympic sporting events of the 2008 Beijing Games have been confirmed under the principle of "safety, quality, construc- tion time, function and cost." Most are under construction or will be by the end of 2005. Other Games venues include Qingdao, (sailing competitions), and Shanghai, Shenyang, Tianjin and Qinghuangdao (all hosts to the football competitions). In addition, on July 8, 2005, the International Olympic Committee announced that equestrian events of the 2008 Games will be held in Hong Kong.

Of the 31 competition venues in Beijing, 11 are new; 11 will use existing facilities, which will be renovated or expanded; nine will be used temporary only. 41 training venues and five facilities that are di- rectly related to the Olympic Games will be needed. To ensure easy access to the Beijing venues, 59 roads and three bridges will be built or renovated.

The construction of 14 venues, eight of them completely new ven- ues, two others that require renovation and five temporary venues will begin in 2005. Some venues will have to be finished by the end of 2006 to hold international competitions, and by the end of 2007, all other venues and related facilities will be finished to hold "test" events.

The construction of eight new venues is in full swing in Beijing. They are the National Stadium, the National Aquatics Centre, the Beijing Shooting Range Hall, the Laoshan Velodrome, the Wukesong Indoor Stadium, the National Indoor Stadium, the China Agriculture University Gymnasium and the Beijing University of Technology Gym- nasium. The remaining three will be launched in the third quarter of 2005.

Organizers of four of the five Olympic facilities, the National Con- vention Centre, the Digital Beijing Building, the Olympic Village and the Olympic Park, have held foundation-stones-laying ceremonies. Con- struction of the Media Village will begin during 2005.

People's Olympics

The last theme of the 2008 Olympic Games, the People's Olympics, is a humanistic principle that shows how truly meaningful this opportunity is for the Chinese people. The people have demonstrated again and again their eagerness to get involved. Genuine displays of affection and national pride followed the Olympic Flame during the Olympic Torch Relay in Beijing in June 2004. This further encouraged ordinary people from all over China to get involved. High participation levels have been seen in various Olympic fund-raising and other supportive events.

On July 13, 2004, the third anniversary of Beijing's winning bid to host the Olympic Games, BOCOG launched the emblem for the 13th Paralympic Games to be held in Beijing shortly after the Summer Olympic Games.

In addition, the Beijing Olympic Broadcasting (BOB) Corporation Limited, the company formed to manage Olympic broadcasts, was officially launched on October 28, 2004. Four days later, on November 1, the Beijing Olympic Media Centre was opened to begin assisting the media in reporting authoritative and regular news about Beijing's Olympic progress and activities.

BOCOG received 20,161 pieces of mail concerning the Beijing 2008 Olympic slogan, and 662 Olympic mascot designs were sent to BOCOG by December 1, 2004. The mascot will be announced sometime this year. In addition, a search for proposals for the best-ever opening and closing ceremonies began on March 1, 2005. Many world famous directors, such as Zhang Yimou and Steven Spielberg, showed great interest in designing the opening and closing ceremonies.

The city launched its volunteer recruiting programme for the 2008 Olympic Games on June 5, 2005. It has also launched a three-year campaign to improve residents' manners to prepare them for the 2008 Olympic Games. Topics to be covered include manners in daily life and social situations, on sports grounds, at work and at school, as well as etiquette in dealing with foreign cultures.

Beijing Partners Club for the 2008 Olympics was established in February 2005. Eighteen domestic and foreign enterprises have joined in the club.

There are more than 1,000 registered athletes in Beijing, and 1,229 new keep-fit programmes were established in 2004. BOCOG welcomes people from the world of sport and ordinary people to get involved.

Telephone Numbers

Hotels

★ ★ ★ ★ ★

Beijing Hotel
北京饭店
📠 33 East Chang'an Jie, Dongcheng District
东城区东长安街 33 号
☎ +86 10 6513 7766

Grand Hotel Beijing
北京贵宾楼饭店
📠 35 East Chang'an Jie, Dongcheng District
东城区东长安街 35 号
☎ +86 10 6513 7788

Hilton Hotel Beijing
北京希尔顿饭店
📠 1 Dongfang Lu, Dongsanhuan Beilu,Chaoyang District
朝阳区东三环北路东方路号
☎ +86 10 6466 2288

Beijing Kempinski Hotel
凯宾斯基饭店
📠 50 Liangmaqiao Lu, Chaoyang District
朝阳区亮马桥路 50 号
☎ +86 10 6465 3388

China World Hotel
中国大饭店
📠 1 Jianguomenwai Dajie, Chaoyang District
朝阳区建国门外大街 1 号
☎ +86 10 6505 2266

Diaoyutai State Guest House
钓鱼台国宾馆
📠 2 Fucheng Lu, Haidian District
海淀区阜成路 2 号
☎ +86 10 6859 1188

Great Wall Sheraton Hotel
长城饭店
📠 10 Dongsanhuan Beilu, Chaoyang District
朝阳区东三环北路 10 号
☎ +86 10 6590 5566

Jing Guang New World Hotel
京广新世界饭店
📠 Hujialou, Chaoyang District
朝阳区呼家楼
☎ +86 10 6597 8888

Kunlun Hotel
昆仑饭店
📠 2 Xinyuan Nanlu, Chaoyang District
朝阳区新源南路 2 号
☎ +86 10 6590 3388

Hotel New Otani Chang Fu Gong
长富宫饭店
📠 26 Jianguomenwai Dajie, Chaoyang District
朝阳区建国门外大街 26 号
☎ +86 10 6512 5555

Peninsula Palace Hotel
王府饭店
📠 8 Goldfish Lane, Wangfujing, DongchengDistrict
王府井金鱼胡同 8 号
☎ +86 10 6559 2888

Shangri-la Hotel Beijing
北京香格里拉饭店
📠 29 Zizhuyuan Lu, Haidian District
海淀区紫竹院路 29 号
☎ +86 10 6841 2211

Grand Hyatt Beijing
北京东方君悦大酒店
📠 1 East Chang'an Jie, Dongcheng District
东城区东长安街 1 号
☎ +86 10 8518 1234

The St. Regis Beijing
北京国际俱乐部饭店
📠 21 Jianguomenwai Dajie, Chaoyang District
朝阳区建国门外大街 21 号
☎ +86 10 6460 6688

Beijing Kerry Center Hotel
北京嘉里中心饭店
📠 1 Guanghua Lu, Chaoyang District
朝阳区光华路 1 号
☎ +86 10 6561 8833

Great Dragon Hotel
兆龙饭店
📠 2 Gongti Beilu, Chaoyang District
朝阳区工体北路 2 号
☎ +86 10 6597 2299

Swissôtel

(Hong Kong-Macau Center)
北京港澳中心瑞士酒店
📠 Dongsishitiao Flyover, Dongcheng District
东城区东四十条立交桥
☎ +86 10 6501 2288

International Hotel
国际饭店
📠 9 Jianguomennei Dajie, Dongcheng District
东城区建内大街 9 号
☎ +86 10 6512 6688

New Century Hotel
新世纪饭店
📠 6 Shouti Nanlu, Haidian District
海淀区首都南路 6 号
☎ +86 10 6849 2001

Crowne Plaza Hotel Beijing
国际艺苑皇冠饭店
📠 48 Wangfujing Dajie, Dongcheng District
东城区王府井大街 48 号
☎ +86 10 6513 3388

Prime Hotel
华侨大厦
📠 2 Wangfujing Dajie, Dongcheng District
东城区王府井大街 2 号
☎ +86 10 6513 6666

Jingrui Hotel
京瑞大厦
📠 17 Dongsanhuan Nanlu, Chaoyang District
朝阳区东三环南路 17 号
☎ +86 10 6766 8866

Beijing Telecom Hotel
京都信苑饭店
📠 6 Shifangyuan, Haidian District
海淀区什坊院 6 号
☎ +86 10 6390 1166

Xiyuan Hotel
西苑饭店
📠 1 Sanlihe Lu, Haidian District
海淀区三里河路 1 号
☎ +86 10 6831 3388

Crowne Plaza Park View Wuzhou Beijing
北京五洲皇冠假日酒店
📠 8 North Fourth Ring Road(M), Chaoyang

Telephone Numbers

District
朝阳区北四环中路8号
☎ +86 10 8498 2288

Days Hotel and Suites Beijing
长安戴斯大饭店
🏨 27 Huaweixili,
Chaoyang District
朝阳区华威里27号
☎ +86 10 6773 1234

Loong Palace Hotel & Resort
龙城丽宫国际酒店
🏨 Huilongguan,
Changping District
昌平区回龙观
☎ +86 10 8079 9988

★ ★ ★ ★

Landmark Towers
亮马河大厦
🏨 8 Dongsanhuan Beilu,
Chaoyang District
朝阳区东三环北路8号
☎ +86 10 6590 6688

CTS Plaza
中旅大厦
🏨 2 Beisanhuan Donglu,
Chaoyang District
朝阳区北三环东路2号
☎ +86 10 6462 2288

Sino-Swiss Hotel
北京国都大饭店
🏨 Xiaotianzhu, Shunyi
District
顺义区小天竺
☎ +86 10 6456 5588

Tianlun Dynasty Hotel
天伦王朝饭店
🏨 50 Wangfujing Dajie,
Dongcheng District
东城区王府井大街50号
☎ +86 10 6513 8888

Jinglun Hotel
京伦饭店
🏨 3 Jianguomenwai
Dajie, Chaoyang
District
朝阳区建国门外大街3号
☎ +86 10 6500 2266

Capital Hotel
首都大酒店
🏨 3 Qianmen Dongdajie,
Chongwen District
崇文区前门东大街3号
☎ +86 10 6512 9988

Radisson SAS Hotel
北京皇家大饭店
🏨 6 Beisanhuan Donglu,
Chaoyang District
朝阳区北三环东路甲6号
☎ +86 10 6466 3388

China Resources Hotel
华润饭店
🏨 35 Jianguo Lu,
Chaoyang District
朝阳区建国路35号
☎ +86 10 8577 2233

Continental Grand Hotel
五洲大酒店
🏨 8 Beichen Donglu,
Andingmenwai,
Chaoyang District
朝阳区安外北辰东路8号
☎ +86 10 6491 5588

Fragrant Hills Hotel
香山饭店
🏨 Inside Fragrant Hills
Park, Haidian District
海淀香山公园内
☎ +86 10 6259 1166

Gloria Plaza Hotel
凯莱大酒店
🏨 2 Jianguomennan
Dajie, Chaoyang
District
建国门南大街2号
☎ +86 10 6515 8855

Rosedale Hotels & Resorts
北京珀丽酒店
🏨 8 Jiangtai Xilu,
Chaoyang District
朝阳区将台西路8号
☎ +86 10 6436 2288

Friendship Hotel
友谊宾馆
🏨 3 Baishiqiao Lu,
Haidian District
海淀区中关村南大街号
☎ +86 10 6849 8888

Holiday Inn Lido Beijing
丽都假日饭店
🏨 Jiangtai Lu, Jichang
Lu, Chaoyang District
朝阳机场路将台路东城区
☎ +86 10 6437 6688

Jianguo Hotel
建国饭店
🏨 5 Jianguomenwai
Dajie, Chaoyang

District
朝阳区建国门外大街5号
☎ +86 10 6500 2233

Xindadu Hotel
新大都饭店
🏨 21 Chegongzhuang
Dajie
西城区车公庄大街21号
☎ +86 10 6831 9988

Novotel Peace Hotel
和平宾馆
🏨 3 Goldfish Lane,
Dongcheng District
东城区金鱼胡同3号
☎ +86 10 6512 8833

Traders Hotel
国贸饭店
🏨 1 Jianguomenwai
Dajie, Chaoyang
District
朝阳区建国门外大街1号
☎ +86 10 6505 2277

Central Garden Hotel
中苑宾馆
🏨 18 Gaoliangqiao
Xiejie,
Haidian District
海淀区高梁桥斜街18号
☎ +86 10 6217 8888

Scitech Hotel
赛特饭店
🏨 22 Jianguomenwai
Dajie, Chaoyang
District
朝阳区建国门外大街
22号
☎ +86 10 6512 3388

Yuyang Hotel
渔阳饭店
🏨 18 Xinyuanxili
Zhongjie,
Chaoyang District
朝阳区新源西里中街
18号
☎ +86 10 6466 9988

Henan Mansion
河南大厦
🏨 28 Huaweili,
Panjiayuan,
Chaoyang District
朝阳区潘家园华威里
28号
☎ +86 10 6775 1188

Yanshan Hotel
燕山大酒店
🏠 A138 Haidianlu,
Haidian District
海淀路甲 138 号
☎ +86 10 6256 3388

Grand View Garden Hotel
北京大观园酒店
🏠 88 Nancaiyuan,
Xuanwu District
宣武区南菜园 88 号
☎ +86 10 6353 8899

Jintai Hotel
金台饭店
🏠 22 Di'anmen Xidajie,
Dongcheng District
东城地安门西大街 22 号
☎ +86 10 6309 9111

Debao Hotel
德宝饭店
🏠 22 Debao Xinyuan,
Xicheng District
西城德宝新园 22 楼
☎ +86 10 6831 8866

New World
CourtyardHotel
新世界万怡酒店
🏠 C, 3 Chongwenmenwai
Dajie, Chongwen District
崇文区崇外大街 3 号 C
☎ +86 10 6708 1188

Poly Plaza
保利大厦
🏠 14 Dongzhimennan
Dajie, Dongcheng
District
东城区东直门南大街
14 号
☎ +86 10 6500 1188

Oriental Garden Hotel
东方花园饭店
🏠 6 Dongzhimennan
Dajie, Dongcheng
District
东城区东直门南大街 6 号
☎ +86 10 6416 8866

Moon River Holiday
Resort
月亮河度假村
🏠 1Yuelianghe Binhe
Lu,Tongzhou District
通州区月亮河滨河路 1 号
☎ +86 10 8952 3737

Minzu Hotel
民族饭店

🏠 51 Fuxingmennei
Dajie, Xicheng District
西城区复兴门内大街
51 号
☎ +86 10 6601 4466

Holiday Inn Downtown Beijing
金都假日饭店
🏠 98 Beilishi Lu,
Xicheng District
西城区北礼士路 98 号
☎ +86 10 6833 8822

Guangzhou Hotel
广州大厦
🏠 3A, Heng Er Tiao,
Xidan,Xicheng District
西城区西单横二条甲 3 号
☎ +86 10 6607 8866

Shenzhen Mansion
深圳大厦
🏠 1 Guang'anmenwai
Dajie, Xuanwu District
宣武区广安门外大街 1 号
☎ +86 10 6327 1188

Holiday Inn Chang An
West Beijing
北京长峰假日酒店
🏠 66 Yongdinglu,
Haidian District
海淀区永定路 66 号
☎ +86 10 6813 2299

Municipal Government Departments

Foreign Affairs Office
北京市人民政府外事办公室
🏠 2 Zhengyi Lu,
Dongcheng District
东城区正义路 2 号
☎ +86 10 6519 2708
🌐 www. bjfao.gov.cn

Office of Overseas
Chinese Affairs
北京市人民政府侨务办公室
🏠 Guanhua Mansion
118 Xizhimennei
Dajie, Xicheng District
西城区西直门内大街
118 号冠华大厦
☎ +86 10 6600 1088
🌐 www.bjqb.gov.cn

Office of Taiwan Affairs
北京市人民政府台湾事务办公室
🏠 Room 322, Donglian
Mansion,

Deshengmendong
Dajie, Xicheng District
西城区德胜门东大街东
联大厦 322 室
☎ +86 10 8408 0909

Beijing Customs
北京海关
🏠 A 10 Guanghua Lu,
Chaoyang District
朝阳区光华路甲 10 号
☎ +86 10 6539 6114
🌐 www.bjcustoms.gov.cn

Beijing Import & Export
Commodity Inspection
Bureau
北京市出入境检验检疫局
🏠 6 Tianshuiyuan Jie,
Chaoyang District
朝阳区甜水园街 6 号
☎ +86 10 5861 9111

Entry & Exit Control Office
of Municipal Security
Bureau
北京市公安局出入境管理处
🏠 2 Andingmen
Dongdajie,
Dongcheng District
东城区安定门东大街 2 号
☎ +86 10 8402 0101

Offices of International Organizations

European Union
Delegation
of the European
Commission
欧洲联盟委员会驻华代表团
🏠 15 Dongzhimenwai Dajie,
Chaoyang District
朝阳区东直门外大街
15 号
☎ +86 10 6532 4443

Offices of Organizations
of the United Nations
System
联合国系统组织代表机构
🏠 2 Liangmahe Nanlu,
Chaoyang District
朝阳区亮马河南路 2 号
☎ +86 10 6532 3731

United Nations
Development Programme
(UNDP)
联合国开发计划署驻华代
表处
🏠 2 Liangmahe Nanlu,
Chaoyang District

Telephone Numbers

朝阳区亮马河南路 2 号
☎ +86 10 6532 3732

Food and Agriculture
Organization of the United
Nations (FAO)
联合国粮食及农业组织驻华代表处
🖂 4-2-151
Jianguomenwai Dajie,
Chaoyang District
朝阳区建国门外大街外
交公寓 4 号楼 2 单元
151 号
☎ +86 10 6532 2835

United Nations Population
Fund (UNFPA)
联合国人口基金会驻华代表处
🖂 1-16-1 Tayuan
Diplomatic Service
Office Building, 14
Liangmahe Nanlu,
Chaoyang District
朝阳区亮马河南路 14 号
塔园外交办公楼 1-16-1
☎ +86 10 6532 3733

World Food Programme
(WFP)
世界粮食计划署驻华代表处
🖂 2 Liangmahe Nanlu,
Chaoyang District
朝阳区亮马河南路 14 号
☎ +86 10 6532 3734

United Nations Children

Fund (UNICEF)
联合国儿童基金会驻华办事处
🖂 12 Sanlitun Lu,
Chaoyang District
朝阳区三里屯路 12 号
☎ +86 10 6532 3131

World Health Organization
(WHO)
世界卫生组织驻华代表处
🖂 9-2-151 Tayuan
Diplomatic Apartments,
1 Xindong Lu,
Dongzhimenwai,
Chaoyang District
朝阳区东直门外新东路
1 号塔园外交公寓 9-2-
151
☎ +86 10 6532 5633

United Nations
Educational,
Scientific and Cultural
Organization (UNESCO)
联合国教科文组织驻华代表处
🖂 153, Building 5,
Jianguomenwai Dajie,
Chaoyang District
朝阳区建国门外大街外
交公寓 5 号楼 153 号
☎ +86 10 6532 1725

International Labour
Organization (ILO)
国际劳工组织北京局
🖂 10/F, Tayuan
Diplomatic Service
Office Building,
Chaoyang District
朝阳区亮马河南路 14
号塔园外交办公楼 10 层
☎ +86 10 6532 5093/4

The World Bank Resident
Mission in China (RMC)
世界银行驻华代表处
🖂 9.F, Tower A, Fuhua
Mansion, 8
Chaoyangmen Bei
Dajie
朝阳门北大街 8 号富华
大厦 A 座 9 层
☎ +86 10 5861 7600

International Monetary
Fund
国际货币基金组织驻华代表处
🖂 Rm. 3612, CWTC
Tower 2, 1
Jianguomenwai Dajie,
Chaoyang District
朝阳区建国门外大街 1 号
国贸大厦 2 座 3612 室
☎ +86 10 6505 1155

Foreign Embassies

Argentina
阿根廷
🖂 11 Sanlitun Dongwujie,
Chaoyang District
朝阳区三里屯东 5 街
11 号
☎ +86 10 6532 1406

Australia
澳大利亚
🖂 21 Dongzhimenwai
Dajie, Chaoyang
District
朝阳区东直门外大街 21 号
☎ +86 10 5140 4111
🌐 www.austemb.org.cn

Austria
奥地利
🖂 5 Xiushui Nanjie,
Jianguomenwai,
Chaoyang District
朝阳区建国门外秀水南
街 5 号
☎ +86 10 6532 2061

Brazil
巴西
🖂 27 Guanghua Lu,
Chaoyang District
朝阳区光华路 27 号
☎ +86 10 6532 2881

Canada
加拿大
🖂 19 Dongzhimenwai
Dajie, Chaoyang District
朝阳区东直门外大街
19 号
☎ +86 10 6532 3536
🌐 www.canada.org.cn

Denmark
丹麦
🖂 1 Sanlitun Dongwujie,
Chaoyang District
朝阳区三里屯东 5 街
1 号
☎ +86 10 6532 2431

Egypt
埃及
🖂 2 Ritan Donglu,
Chaoyang District
朝阳区日坛东路 2 号
☎ +86 10 6532 1825

Finland
芬兰
🖂 26/F, Beijing Kerry
Center, South Tower, 1
Guanghualu,
Chaoyang District
朝阳区光华路 1 号嘉里
中心南楼 26 层
☎ +86 10 8529 8541
🌐 http://www.finland-in-
china.com

France
法国
🖂 3 Sanlitun Dongsanjie,
Chaoyang District
朝阳区三里屯东 3 街
3 号
☎ +86 10 8532 8080
🌐 www.dree.org/china

Germany
德国
☎ 17 Dongzhimenwai Dajie, Chaoyang District
朝阳区东直门外大街17号
☏ +86 10 8532 9000
ⓘ www.deutschebotschaft-china.org

Italy
意大利
☎ 2 Sanlitun Dong'erjie, Chaoyang District
朝阳区三里屯东2街2号
☏ +86 10 6532 2131
ⓘ www.italianembassy.org.cn

Japan
日本
☎ 7 Ritan Lu, Jianguomenwai, Chaoyang District
朝阳区建国门外日坛路7号
☏ +86 10 6532 2361
ⓘ www.japan.org.cn

Korea
韩国
☎ 3 Sanlitun Dongsijie, Chaoyang District
朝阳区三里屯东4街3号
☏ +86 10 6532 0290
ⓘ www.koreaemb.org.cn

Netherlands
荷兰
☎ 4 Liangmahe Nanlu, Chaoyang District
朝阳区亮马河南路4号
☏ +86 10 6532 1131
ⓘ www.nlembassypek.org

Portugal
葡萄牙
☎ 8 Sanlitun Dongwujie, Chaoyang District
朝阳区三里屯东5街8号
☏ +86 10 6532 3497

Russia
俄罗斯
☎ 4 Dongzhimen Beizhongjie, Dongcheng District
东城区东直门北中街4号

☏ +86 10 6532 1381
ⓘ www.russia.org.cn

Singapore
新加坡
☎ 7/F, North Tower, Beijing Kerry Center, 1 Guanghualu, Chaoyang District
朝阳区光华路1号北京嘉里中心北楼7层
☏ +86 10 6532 1115
ⓘ www.mfa.gov.sg/beijing

South Africa
南非
☎ 5 Dongzhimenwai Dajie, Chaoyang District
朝阳区东直门外大街5号
☏ +86 10 6532 0171

Spain
西班牙
☎ 9 Sanlitun Donglu, Chaoyang District
朝阳区三里屯东路9号
☏ +86 10 6532 1986

United Kingdom
英国
☎ 11 Guanghua Lu, Chaoyang District
朝阳区光华路11号
☏ +86 10 5192 4000
ⓘ www.britishembassy.org.cn

United States
美国
☎ 3 Xiushui Beijie, Jianguomenwai, Chaoyang District
朝阳区建国门外秀水北街3号
☏ +86 10 6532 3831
ⓘ www.usembassy- china.org.cn

International Clinics

Peking Union Medical College Hospital, Foreigners' Emergency Clinic
北京协和医院
☎ 53 Dongdanbei Dajie, Dongcheng District
东城区东单北大街53号
☏ +86 10 6529 5269

China-Japan Friendship Hospital
中日友好医院
☎ Yinghua Dong Lu,

Hepingjie Beikou, Chaoyang District
朝阳区和平街北口樱花东路
☏ +86 10 6422 2952

International Medical Center (IMC)
北京国际医疗中心
☎ Room S 106, Beijing Lufthansa Center, 50 Liangmaqiao Lu, Chaoyang District
朝阳区亮马桥路50号北京燕莎中心S106室
☏ +86 10 6465 1561/62

International SOS
北京国际救援中心
☎ Building C, BITIC Leasing Center, 1 Xingfusancun Beilu, Chaoyang District
朝阳区幸福三村北路1号北信租赁中心C座
☏ +86 10 6462 9112 for clinic appointment, 6462 9100 for 24-hour alarm line, 6462 0555 for general information

Hong Kong International Medical Clinic
北京香港国际医务诊所
☎ 9/F, Hong Kong-Macau Center, 2 Chaoyangmenbei Dajie, Dongcheng District
东城区朝阳门北大街2号港澳 中心9层
☏ +86 10 6553 2288, ext. 2345/ 2346/2347

Beijing United Family Hospital
和睦家医院
☎ 2 Jiangtai Lu, Chaoyang District
朝阳区将台路2号
☏ +86 10 6433 3961

Bayley & Jackson Medical Group
庇利积臣医疗中心
☎ 7 Ritandong Lu, Chaoyang District
朝阳区日坛路7号
☏ +86 10 8562 9998

Telephone Numbers

Guree Dental
固瑞齿科
- NB 210 China World Trade Center, Chaoyang District
  朝阳区建国门外大街 1 号国贸商城 NB210
- ☎ +86 10 6505 9439

Wista Clinic
维世达诊所
- B29 Kerry Center, 1 Guanghua Lu, Chaoyang District
  朝阳区光华路 1 号嘉里中心 B29
- ☎ +86 10 8529 6618

International Schools

Beijing City International School
北京乐成国际学校
- 77 Baiziwan Nan Er Lu, Chaoyang District
  朝阳区百子湾南 2 路
- ☎ +86 10 8771 7171

Beijing International BISS School
北京 BISS 国际学校
- Building 17, Area 4, An Zhen Xi Li, Chaoyang District
  朝阳区安贞里西 4 区 17 楼
- ☎ +86 10 6443 3151/2

Japanese School of Beijing
北京日本人学校
- 6 Jiangtai Xilu, Chaoyang District
  朝阳区将台西路 6 号
- ☎ +86 10 6436 3250

Indian Embassy School
印度学校
- 1 Ritan Donglu, Chaoyang District
  朝阳区日坛东路 1 号
- ☎ +86 10 6532 1827

French Embassy School
法国学校
- 13 Sanlitun Dongsijie, Chaoyang District
  朝阳区三里屯东四街 13 号
- ☎ +86 10 6532 3498

German Embassy School
德国学校
- 49A Liangmaqiao Lu, Chaoyang District
  朝阳区亮马桥路甲 49 号
- ☎ +86 10 6532 2535

International School of Beijing- Shunyi
北京顺义国际学校
- 10, Anhua Street, Shunyi District
  顺义区安华街 10 号
- ☎ +86 10 8149 2345

Western Academy of Beijing
北京京西学校
- 10 Laiguangying Donglu, Chaoyang District
  朝阳区来广营东路 10 号
- ☎ +86 10 8456 4155

Australian International School Beijing (AISB)
北京澳大利亚国际学校
- 7 Louzizhuang Lu, Chaoyang District
  朝阳区楼梓庄路 7 号
- ☎ +86 10 8439 4405

Eton International School
伊顿国际学校
- No.8 South Road Sun Park, Chaoyang District
  朝阳公园南路 8 号棕泉国际公寓
- ☎ +86 10 6539 8967
- ✉ info@etonkids.com

The British School of Beijing 北京英国学校
- 5 Sanlitun Xi Liujie, Chaoyang district
  朝阳区三里屯西六街 5 号
- ☎ +86 10 8532 3088

Swedish School Beijing
北京瑞典学校
- Legend Garden Villa, 89 Capital Airport Road
  朝阳区机场路 89 号
- ☎ +86 10 6456 0826

The New School of Collaborative Learning (NSCL)
北京协力国际学校
- An Ning Zhuang, Haidian District
  海淀区清河镇安宁庄北京供电技校内
- ☎ +86 10 6298 5758

Beijing Huijia Private School
北京市私立汇佳学校
- Zhongguancun Technology Garden, Changping Garden
  海淀区中关村科技园昌平园
- ☎ +86 10 6974 4795

Beijing Qiao Zhi Bo Ren Kindergarten
北京乔治布朗国际幼儿园
- 1/F, North Apartment, China World Trade Center, 1 Jianguomenwai, Chaoyang District
  朝阳区建国门外 1 号国贸中心北公寓一层
- ☎ +86 10 6505 3869

Yew Chung Beijing International School
北京耀中国际学校
- East Gate of Honglingjin Park, 5 Houbalizhuang, Chaoyang District
  朝阳区后八里庄 5 号红领巾公园东门
- ☎ +86 10 8583 3731

Korea International School in Beijing
北京韩国国际学校
- 531 Qiliqu, Changping District
  昌平区七里渠 531 号
- ☎ +86 10 8072 4526/27

International Department of Beijing Huiwen High School
北京汇文中学国际部
- 6 Peixin Jie, Chongwen District
  崇文区培新街 6 号
- ☎ +86 10 6712 4120

Beijing Fangcaodi Primary School
北京市朝阳区芳草地小学
- 1 Ritan Beilu, Chaoyang District
  朝阳区日坛北路 1 号
- ☎ +86 10 8563 5120

Lido Kindergarten Beijing
北京丽都幼儿园
- Jichang Lu, Jiangtai
  Lu, Chaoyang District
  朝阳区将台路
- +86 10 6437 6688,
  ext. 1640

Beijing Oxford Little
Professor Kindergarten
北京小牛津双语幼儿园
- 308 Building,
  Huizhongli, Asian
  Games Village,
  Chaoyang District
  朝阳区亚运村慧忠里
  308 楼
- +86 10 6493 6626

The International
Montessori School of
Beijing
蒙台梭利幼儿园
- 7 Sanlitun Beixiaojie,
  Chaoyang District
  朝阳区三里屯北小街7号
- +86 10 6532 6713

Beijing Zhongguancun
International School
中关村国际学校
- Building 14, Taiyangyuan,
  Dazhongsi, Haidian
  District
  海淀区大钟寺太阳园
  14 号楼
- +86 10 8213 8339

Places to
Learn Chinese

Beijing Chinese School
北京中文学校
- 23/F, Tower A, CITIC
  Building, 19
  Jianguomenwai Dajie,
  Chaoyang District
  朝阳区建外大街 19 号
  国际大厦 A 座 23 层
- +86 10 8526 2417

Peking University
北京大学
- 5 Yiheyuan Lu,
  Haidian District
  海淀区颐和园路 5 号
- +86 10 6275 1230

Tsinghua Universit
清华大学
- Tsinghua University,
  Haidian District

海淀区清华大学
- +86 10 6278 4857

University of International
Business and Economics
对外经济贸易大学
- 12 Huixin Dongjie,
  Chaoyang District
  朝阳区惠新东街 12 号
- +86 10 6449 2329

Renmin Univeristy of
China
人民大学
- Zhongguancun Dajie,
  Haidian District
  海淀区中关村大街
- +86 10 6251 1588

Beijing Foreign Studies
University
北京外国语大学
- 2 Xisanhuan Beilu,
  Haidian District
  海淀区西三环北路 2 号
- +86 10 6891 6549,
  6894 5373

Beijing University of
Science and Technology
北京科技大学
- 30 Xueyuanlu, Haidian
  District
  海淀区学院路 30 号
- +86 10 6233 2942

Beijing Language and
Culture University
北京语言大学
- 15 Xueyuanlu,
  Haidian District
  海淀区学院路 15 号
- +86 10 8230 3928

Beijing Normal University
北京师范大学
- 19 Xinjiekouwai Dajie,
  Haidian District
  海淀区新街口外大街
  19 号
- +86 10 6220 7986

Fitness Clubs

Powerland Fitness Centre
葆莱健身中心
- 3 Xiaoyun Lu,
  Chaoyang District
  朝阳区霄云路 3 号
- +86 10 8454 5500
  Programmes:
  Taekwondo, fitness,

aerobics, shaping,
yoga, massage

Beijing Evolution Fitness
Centre
北京进步健身中心
- Da Bei Yao Property
  Center, 2 (S) East
  Third Ring Road,
  Chaoyang District
  朝阳区大北窑东三环南
  路 2 号大北窑物业中心
- +86 10 6567 0266
  Programmes:
  aerobics, shaping,
  yoga, boxing, street
  dance

Nirvana Fitness Club
北京青鸟健身中心
- The west building of
  Great Dragon Hotel, 2
  Gongtibei Lu,
  Chaoyang District
  朝阳区工体北路 2 号兆
  龙饭店西楼
- +86 10 6597 2008/9
  Programmes:
  Taekwondo, boxing,
  fitness, aerobics,
  shaping, yoga, ballet,
  weight losing,
  massage

Bally Total Fitness
中体倍力健身中心
- W/1, Chang'an Grand
  Theater, 7
  Jianguomennei Dajie,
  Dongcheng District
  东城区建国门内大街 7
  号长安大戏院地下一层
- +86 10 6518 1666
  Programmes:
  pilates, boxercise,
  indoor cycling, yoga,
  tai chi, circuit
  training, express
  exercise

Body Works Fitness
Centre
宝迪沃健身中心
- 5 & 6 th floor, site D,
  Chengming Building,
  2 Xizhimen, Xicheng
  District
  西城区西直门南大街 2 号
  成铭大厦 D 座五、六层
- +86 10 6615 8800
  Programmes:
  swimming, fitness,

Telephone Numbers

shaping, yoga,
massage, sauna

Clark Hatch Life Spa
克拉克海奇健身俱乐部
- 2/F, International
Hotel, 9
Jianguomennei Dajie,
Dongcheng District
东城区建国门内大街 9
号国际饭店二层
- +86 10 6512 6688,
ext.83
Programmes:
swimming, fitness,
massage, sauna,
beauty spa

Lufthansa Centre fitness
Club
燕莎健身中心
- 50 Liangmaqiao Lu,
neighbouring
Kempinski Hotel,
Chaoyang District
朝阳区亮马桥路 50 号
- +86 10 6465 3388,
ext. 5721
Programmes:
tennis, table tennis,
swimming, fitness,
aerobics, yoga, ballet

Kerry Fitness Center
嘉里健身中心
- Kerry Centre Hotel, 1
Guanghua Lu,
Chaoyang District
朝阳区光华路 1 号嘉里
中心饭店内
- +86 10 6561 8833, ext.
6465
Programmes:
table tennis,
badminton,
swimming,
taekwondo, fitness,
aerobics, shaping,
yoga, ballet, massage

Dongdan Sports Center
东单体育中心
- 106
Chongwenmenwai
Dajie, Dongcheng
District
东城区崇文门内大街
106 号
- +86 10 6522 2111
(service); 6512 3326
(bowling); 6559 6164

(table tennis)
Programmes:
tennis, basketball,
table tennis,
badminton, bowling,
swimming, shaping

Yingdong Swimming
Center
英东游泳馆
- inside National
Olympic, Sports
Centre, 1 Andinglu,
Chaoyang District
朝阳区安定路 1 号奥体
中心内
- +86 10 6491 2233,
ext.315
Programmes:
table tennis, billiard,
badminton, bowling,
swimming, fitness,
aerobics

Haosha Bodybuilding
Club
浩沙健身中心
- 2/F, Beijing
Exhibition Theatre,
Xicheng District
西城区北京展览馆二层
- +86 10 6836 8819
Programmes:
table tennis,
badminton, swimming,
taekwondo, fitness,
aerobics, shaping,
yoga

Skating Rinks

LeCool Ice Rink
LeCool 溜冰场
- Basement 2, China
World Shopping Mall,
Chaoyang District
朝阳区国贸商城地下二层
- +86 10 6505 5776

Champion Skating rink
冠军溜冰场
- Basement 1, New
World Shopping Centre,
Chongwen District
崇文区新世界商场二期
地下一层
- +86 10 6708 9523

Zilongxiang Ice Skating
紫龙祥溜冰场
- North Gate of Ditan

Park, 14 Hepingli Zhong
Jie, Chaoyang District
朝阳区和平里中街甲
14 号地坛公园北门
- +86 10 6429 1619

Xidan Ice Rink
西单溜冰场
- Xidan Culture Square,
Xicheng District
西城区西单文化广场
- +86 10 6603 0050

Foot Massage

Emerson Massage
爱博森盲人按摩院
- 11A, Liufang Beili,
Chaoyang District
朝阳区柳芳北里甲 11 号
- +86 10 6465 2044

Daban Foot Massage
大班足疗保健
- 6,7F, Gangmei Dasha,
1Xiaogongfu,Wangfujing
Dajie, Dongcheng
District
东城区王府井大街霞公
府 1 号港美大厦 6，7 层
- +86 10 6512 0868

Tianhe Liangzi
天河良子健身
- 2F, Golden Bridge
Building, 1A
Jianguomenwai Dajie,
Chaoyang District
朝阳区建国门外大街
1 号金之桥大厦 2 层
- +86 10 6507 9285

Tianxingjian Foot
Massage Centre
天行健足底保健中心
- North building, 23
Baiwanzhuang Dajie,
Xicheng District
西城区百万庄大街 23
号北楼
- +86 10 6831 9550

Disco & Karaoke

Melody KTV
麦乐迪 KTV
- 77 Chaoyangmenwai
Dajie, Chaoyang
District

朝阳区朝外大街 77 号
☎ +86 10 6551 0808

Party World KTV
钱柜 KTV
📍 1F, Fanli Building, 22 Chaoyangmenwai Dajie, Chaoyang District
朝阳区朝外大街泛利大厦一层
☎ +86 10 6588 3333
📍 168 Xizhimenwai Dajie, Xicheng District
西城区西直门外大街 168 号
☎ +86 10 8857 6566

Party Life KTV
乐圣 KTV
📍 Zhengren Tower, 9 Chongwenmenwai Dajie, Chongwen District
崇文区崇文门外大街 9 号正仁大厦
☎ +86 10 6708 6666

Libraries

National Library of China
中国国家图书馆
📍 33 Zhongguancun Nan Dajie, Haidian District
海淀区中关村南大街 33 号
☎ +86 10 8854 5426/ 5360
ℹ http://www.nlc.gov.cn

Capital Library
首都图书馆
📍 88 South East Ring Road, Chaoyang District
朝阳区东三环南路 88 号
☎ +86 10 6735 8114

Golf

Beijing CBD Golf Club
北京 CBD 国际高尔夫球俱乐部
📍 99 Gaobeidian Lu, East Fourth Ring Road, Chaoyang District

朝阳区东四环高碑店路 99 号
Holes: 18
☎ +86 10 6738 4809

Beijing Golf Club
北京高尔夫球俱乐部
📍 Shangsi Lu, Tuanjiehu, Chaoyang District
朝阳区团结湖小区上泗路
Holes: 18
☎ +86 10 6515 0812

Beijing Honghua International Golf Club
北京鸿华国际高尔夫球俱乐部
📍 108 Beiyuan Lu, Asian Games Village, Chaoyang District
朝阳区亚运村北苑路 108 号
Hole: 18
☎ +86 10 6496 8363

Beijing International Golf Club
北京国际高尔夫球俱乐部
📍 Ming Tombs Reservoir, Changping District
昌平区十三陵水库北侧
Holes: 18
☎ +86 10 6076 2288

Beijing Jinghua Golf Club
北京京华高尔夫球俱乐部
📍 Yanjiao development zone
燕郊经济开发区
Holes: 36
☎ +86 10 6159 1234

Huatang International Golf Club
华堂国际高尔夫球俱乐部
📍 Yanjiao Development Zone
燕郊经济开发区
Holes: 18
☎ +86 10 6159 3932

Moonriver Golf Recreation Club (Tongzhou):
月亮河休闲俱乐部
📍 1 Hebin Lu, Yuelianghe, Tongzhou District
通州区月亮河滨路 1 号

☎ +86 10 8952 6007/8
ℹ www.moonriver.com.cn

Village Golf Club
乡村高尔夫俱乐部
📍 Mapo, Shunyi County
顺义区马坡地区潮白河
☎ + 86 10 6940 1111, 6940 3788

Children Directory

Baby Angel Photography
宝贝天使专业儿童摄影
📍 0102, 2/F Building 2, SOHO, 39 Dongsanhuan Zhonglu, Chaoyang District
朝阳区东三环中路 39 号建外 SOHO2 号楼 2 层 0102 室
☎ +86 10 5869 3503

Beijing Wildlife Park
北京野生动物园
📍 Donghulin, Daxing Yufa, Daxing County
大兴县大兴榆垡东湖林
☎ +86 10 8921 6666

Beijing Zoo 北京动物园
📍 137 Baishiqiao Lu, Xizhimenwai Dajie, Haidian District
海淀区西外大街白石桥路 137 号
☎ +86 10 6831 4411

Blue Zoo Beijing
富国海底世界
📍 Workers' Stadium South Gate, Chaoyang District
朝阳区工人体育场南门
☎ +86 10 6591 3397

China Puppet Theater
中国木偶剧院
📍 1A, Area 1, Anhua Xili, Beisanhuan Lu, Chaoyang District
朝阳区北三环路安华西里 1 区甲 1 号
☎ +86 10 6422 9487